table life

an invitation to everyday discipleship

GREG MAMULA

Foreword by Scot McKnight

I0807937

JUDSON PRESS
PUBLISHERS SINCE 1824
VALLEY FORGE, PA

Table Life: An Invitation to Everyday Discipleship

Interior design by Crystal Devine.
Cover design by Wendy Ronga, Hampton Design Group.

Library of Congress Cataloging-in-Publication data

Names: Mamula, Greg, author.
Title: Table life : an invitation to everyday discipleship / Greg Mamula ; foreword by Scot McKnight.
Identifiers: LCCN 2020004930 (print) | LCCN 2020004931 (ebook) | ISBN 9780817018153 (paperback) | ISBN 9780817082147 (epub)
Subjects: LCSH: Dinners and dining--Religious aspects--Christianity. | Dinners and dining in the Bible. | Christian life.
Classification: LCC BR115.N87 M36 2020 (print) | LCC BR115.N87 (ebook) | DDC 248.4/6--dc23
LC record available at https://lccn.loc.gov/2020004930
LC ebook record available at https://lccn.loc.gov/2020004931

Printed in the U.S.A.

First printing, 2020.

Contents

Foreword by Scot McKnight v
Preface viii
Acknowledgments xi

CHAPTERS
1. Introduction to Table Life 1
2. How Meals Shape Us 22
3. Shaped by the Narrative 47
4. Listening 65
5. Storytelling 87
6. Communion 107
7. New Media and #tablelife 125
8. Emmaus Journey to the Table 143
9. Final Thoughts 156

APPENDICES
A. Dwelling in the Word 160
B. Storytelling Guide 163
C. Sharing Questions 165
D. Communion Liturgies 170

Bibliography 176

Foreword

Two summers during my college years were spent with a summer evangelistic team in Wiener Neustadt, Austria. My German was challenged to grow *ganz schnell*, which it did, but my Christian growth happened playing a card game called *Dutch Blitz*. After dinner and some light chores, we sat in a large room around tables, talking and playing *Dutch Blitz*. Sometimes we sang and sometimes we prayed, but we mostly chatted with one another about life back home and what we were reading and what we were experiencing going door-to-door in a country not all that hospitable to our ideas. But evenings were our lifeline. They were a lifeline because of the table.

There is something about food and drink and a few people sitting together around a table, without some schedule breathing down our necks or some agenda driving our time. Annually biblical professors gather at a monster meeting called Society of Biblical Literature where we see our friends, when we get to eat together and then talk until we wear down and head to bed. Recently I was talking to a professor friend about what SBL might be like during COVID-19's shutdowns, and he had heard that one suggestion was that it would be online—and my friend said, "What's SBL without seeing our friends and eating with one another?" Exactly. There is something about table fellowship that creates the perfect culture for Christian communion and spiritual growth.

Jesus knew this. His Jewish forebears and his first-century followers knew this. In fact, the entire world knew this until the Industrial Revolution. Until then evenings were about eating, sitting around the table or the garden, and chatting with family and friends and fellow believers. Gospel scholars know that most of Jesus' teachings were responses to questions people asked him, and the most common setting for those questions and responses were evening, after-dinner conversations.

Try reading some Gospel passages and before you begin a passage, imagine Jesus sitting (or reclining) at a table with a half dozen folks doing the same. That's the setting for many of Jesus' teachings. For example, the parable of the Prodigal Son, which is found in Luke 15. This parable is actually the third of three, the first about a lost sheep, the second about a lost coin, and our parable follows those. Why did Jesus tell those parables? Because the theological experts and critics had been watching Jesus, and what they were watching was what he was doing at the table. "The Pharisees and the scribes," Luke 15:2 tells us, "were grumbling" about Jesus because "this fellow welcomes sinners and eats with them." Word on the street about Jesus was that "the Son of Man came eating and drinking," and the charge was that he was a "glutton and a drunkard, a friend of tax collectors and sinners" (Matthew 11:19). Think about it: Jesus' most distinctive teachings about God, about kingdom, and about discipleship were explained and *embodied* at the table.

Greg Mamula knows that the table can be transforming for those who will put down the cell phone, turn off the news cycle, and tune out sports or Netflix, and carve out time to sit and eat with one another and let conversations naturally flow. He knows from his experience in churches that when Christians gather together to read Scripture, pray, and break bread together, they experience a bit of God's kingdom. The kind of kingdom Jesus himself lived and taught.

I watched *Table Life* grow from an idea in Greg's head into a thesis that was well researched and then into a ministry project embodied when Christians gathered at the Table. Greg knows the church is a better place for reconciliation and love, for learning and growth when we do what the apostle Paul once advised the Christians of Rome: "welcome one another, therefore, just as Christ has welcomed you" (Romans 15:7). When you hear that word *welcome*, please don't imagine a visitor coming through the door to your church. Instead, envision yourself sitting down at someone's table for an evening of fellowship. That's what Paul was on about in Romans 14–15 and that's what shaped the ministry of Jesus. May we all join them at the Table.

Scot McKnight
Professor of New Testament
Northern Seminary

Preface

I stumbled into the table life by accident. Table life is a holistic approach to faith and life. Engaging in the mealtime habits of listening, storytelling, reading Scripture as narrative, and communion help us participate in the kingdom of God in our communities. I did not know I wanted or needed it, yet somehow table life found me just the same. Rather than suddenly entering my life all at once, table life gradually appeared until it deeply impacted me. Like any spiritual habit, the impact of table life on me started small. For example, when I received my first paycheck at fifteen, I immediately asked my dad (who drove the car and who hired me to help at his company during the summer) if he would join me for a meal at the nearest restaurant, for table fellowship. Although I don't remember our conversation, I remember feeling closer to him.

In college, I ate every meal with my closest friends. After I married, and my wife and I moved to an off-campus apartment, we often hosted those same friends for dinner. While in seminary, we made a habit of hosting classmates and coworkers on weekends and holidays. By the time graduation arrived, hosting a cookout felt natural. These meals provided the time and space for people to talk about the difficulties of graduate courses, financial struggles, and crises of faith. At the time, we did not understand that these meals were holy encounters.

Over the years I have sat at many dinner tables, banquets, receptions, restaurants, and picnic tables with people from various walks of life. Some meals held particular significance to me, remembering times when I poured my heart out to mentors in a desperate search for guidance, made important family decisions, or received a job. Other meals do not share the same distinctive memories, but gathering at the table with the same people over and over again has fostered deep bonds. I also remember moments of isolation and loneliness, eating meals alone in my dining room, in a car, or while traveling.

A life shaped by the table is one shaped by community. Eating with others is holy work. You share common dishes. You listen to your tablemates' stories and tell yours in turn. You bond over breads, salads, pastas, and desserts. The narrative of our lives begins to intertwine with others' when we eat, pray, and lovingly listen our way forward together. Eating with others satisfies our basic need for nourishment and creates space for holy interaction with the Divine and those made in God's image. Meals are holy because they are a gateway into the deeper mysteries of faith and life.

Once I began to understand meals as the catalyst for bonding and spiritual growth, I began to wonder if there are ways to be more aware and intentional about what takes place between the setting of the table and the washing of dishes. Several years ago, I began to pay attention and ask questions of my dining interactions. I read books and articles about table fellowship, community, the presence of Christ, communion, and listening. I attended conferences and met with practitioners around the table to ask what was working and what needed adjusting. I would experiment with various aspects of those learnings with some church friends and neighbors until our family stumbled into a Table Life.

Table life offers a holistic approach to faith and life as an intentional, interactive process of reflection and action, meals and mission, listening and storytelling, Scripture and perspective, communion and neighboring. It connects individuals with Christ, the local church, their neighborhood, and their community contexts. By participating in the long-practiced spiritual disciplines of eating together, listening, storytelling, reading Scripture, and communion, you begin to recognize and celebrate the presence of Christ in every aspect of life. These disciplines help foster community with the church and the many places we engage in daily.

Jesus chose the symbol of the table to leave to his followers after spending a good portion of his ministry at dinner tables with a variety of people. He spent so much time at the table that he was called a glutton, a drunkard, and a friend of sinners. Perhaps he spent a great deal of time at the table, because the holy and ordinary collide here, a thin space where heaven and earth meet. A dinner table where people gather becomes a communion table full with Jesus' powerful presence. Living a table life reveals Jesus to us, sitting at the head of the table with cup and bread in hand for us to take, eat, remember, and celebrate.

Greg Mamula
March 2020

Acknowledgments

First, I want to thank the many people who have sat at the table with me during my life. Your presence helps me reexamine how I see the world and look for Christ in everyday experiences. In a world where time is as valuable as financial resources, you have given me and my family something precious by investing your time at a table with us. Thank you for sharing your stories, your families, and your love with us. Specifically, I want to thank my dear friends who first intentionally gathered to eat, share stories, and reflect on our spiritual journeys that birthed the concept of table life. To Jeff, Erin, Tyler, Alaina, Jack, and Kim, I am forever grateful for your presence in my life. May Christ continue to reveal himself to you as you engage the world in mission and ministry.

I must also extend gratitude to my neighbors who have become like family to me over the past several years. In his classic poem "Mending Wall," Robert Frost asks why good walls make good neighbors. Fences, gates, and property lines have their place, but I am grateful we often blur the lines or cross them to become an intimate community on top of a small hill at the end of a minor neighborhood street. Thank you to Joel, Michelle, Jack, Luke, Ella, and Annie; Jason and Deanna; Gayle and Mark; Andy, Adriana, Matias, and Ximena; and Andy and Linda for the hours of conversations around grapevines, driveways, and dinner tables. I am blessed and honored to be part of your lives and the love you share with my family.

Thank you to my wife, Lisa, and children, Sophie and Joel. Every day we gather around the table in gratitude. We take turns to pray and talk about our days. We laugh and sometimes grumble, but mostly we are just present with one another. I am so glad to share the table with you every single day. Thank you for leading me in table life.

To the churches and pastors who are trying table life in their congregations, I hope this book helps you foster community that draws the people of God closer to Jesus, the church, and one another. Special thanks are extended to Sunset Hills Baptist Church and Pastor Paul Marine for being the first congregation to put table life into practice. To the many other congregations who have tried table life, blessings on your journeys as you continue to live in fellowship with Christ and one another.

A special word of thanks must go to Dr. Scot McKnight, who encouraged and challenged me to write. Thank you for believing in me and guiding me through the rough places. You and my fellow DMin cohort members see things in me I don't readily see in myself. Thank you for challenging me to work on this project and get it finished. Thank you for continuing to be in my life even though we graduated and are involved in our various works of ministry.

To my spiritual director, Jeff Savage, thank you for your constant presence and encouragement. Your timely questions and insights continue to challenge me to ask questions about my faith journey and table ministry. Your wisdom and council are precious to me.

Finally, to Judson Press and their team of editors, without you nobody would have a book to hold or content to download onto tablets. I am grateful for your willingness to engage in this journey with me.

1

Introduction to Table Life

Community participation does not come naturally to many of us. Developing stronger communities requires engaging in habits designed to draw you closer to God, your church, and the people in your community. Practicing discipleship habits that foster spiritual and community growth challenges the individualistic instinct in each of us. Practicing these types of habits also cannot be done in a vacuum. For personal spiritual growth and communal spiritual growth to occur, these habits must be practiced in the context of a community. They help you listen for and discern God's presence in your life, church, and community and, in their holistic approach, can be integrated into the ordinariness of life.

This book is an invitation to join your brothers and sisters in Christ around the table to eat together, dwell in the Word,[1] share stories, listen, and share communion. You are invited into Table Life.

Table Life Is Rooted in Community

Table life actively searches for the presence of Christ in the most ordinary, daily activities: "Eating is a sacred business.

Whether it's eggs on toast in a café, cornflakes scarfed down at the kitchen bench, a sandwich shared with colleagues in the cafeteria, or a leisurely family dinner at the dining room table, eating is a spiritual act."[2] This view of eating seems mysterious; however, when we stop and ponder the impact meals have on our lives, we discover that eating is one of our most meaningful activities, "one so immersed in human longing and relationship that it's a practice of sacred dimensions."[3]

It is important to value the ordinary things in our lives. Every year since 2001 the *MIT Technology Review* reveals its top ten breakthrough technologies of the year. These breakthroughs are technological advances that have deep impact on our lives.[4] Things that quickly become commonplace—like wireless networks, facial recognition, universal authentication, self-driving vehicles, solar and wind energy, genome and genetic mapping, and cloud streaming—have all made the list. These breakthrough technologies and their adoption into mainstream use are examples of how quickly change happens in our world. We live in an amazing age of advancement. But what has been lost?

In an age of rapid change, social media alerts, disjointed schedules, and constant digital connection, the search for meaningful, intimate communities seems more urgent than ever. Even with advancement all around us we realize how they diminish our meaningful relationships. We long for the "majestic reality of God and the immediate significance of each personal and local detail in the story of redemption . . . the work that has to do with the human's relation to God and God's will for the human does not come from knowing more about the times but from knowing humanity—and God. It has to do with continuities, not novelties; with what is essential in the human condition, not what is accidental."[5] Deep relationships allow people and communities to thrive and speak to an essential part of humanity.

We desperately need substance, not another program that encourages shallow relationships. We need connection to the divine, to other people, and to the ordinary. A table life centered around meals, listening, storytelling, the narrative of Scripture, and communion helps foster such connections. The table calls us to sit with others and concerns "such fundamentally human things as intimacy and family, identity and communication, reconciliation and romance, covenant and community, redemption and friendship, sustenance and celebration, beginnings and endings."[6] Tables are the only thing strong enough to hold every aspect of our lives.

Table Life in the Everyday

A retired farmer in a rural church with declining attendance rates started to think about ways his struggling church could better connect with his community. Like many rural churches, his church consisted of long-time members, declining in health due to years spent hard at work in corn fields, running small businesses, and the effects of aging in general. These members love Jesus and were active in this local church for their entire lives, but recently they lost their ability and desire to start new ministries in the church and engage in civic activities in the broader community. Although their ability to get involved decreased, the members hope their church—the one in which they were baptized, married, raised children, helped with mission trips, and served on a variety of boards—offered a place of comfortable familiarity for them and guests. They wanted to see their friends, attend worship, and spend time together at the annual church family picnic. These saints held the story of Christ's presence in their church, town, and county, but became worn out physically, emotionally, and spiritually.

With the help of his pastor, a few good books, and a regional church conference, the farmer explored ways he could get his church friends out of the 100-year-old church building and into the community to meet new people. For his part, he chose to volunteer at the local school sporting events by working the concessions stand. He had long participated in a few local hobby groups and ate his breakfasts in the local coffee shops that dotted the town square. But he had not previously seen those familiar habits as spaces where Christ dwelled; he felt that the church building or even the cab of his tractor, in which he lovingly works the land God had called him to cultivate, reserved Christ's presence. But now he felt less sure of placing this limitation on God. He went for walks around town throughout the day to observe and listen to his surroundings. He started conversations with new people about Christ, which seemed to come naturally to him. In this fresh perspective, he experienced a personal spiritual revival.

The farmer's personal revival started to spread as people who he had spoken to visited the church. In his enthusiasm, he encouraged the church and pastor to organize mid-week events, Bible studies, parent night outs, and game nights with the new visitors in mind. The aging and long-ignored church building found new use. The desire to breathe new life into the church building began to emerge.

After organizing new events, the church members updated the fellowship hall with improved flooring, fresh paint, and better lighting with the help of donations and the church's endowment. The church members contributed to the initial labor and contracted out the remaining portions. This built momentum in the church and soon a monthly outreach ministry that supplied goods for local low-income households developed. On one of his many walks, the farmer noticed a number of single mothers bustling around town getting babies in and out of cars, looking fatigued as they ran necessary errands. The church supplied diapers, formula, clothing, food, and coupon books for stores to give to families with infants and toddlers, hoping this would lessen their load. For the next year, nearly a hundred people came to the church one Saturday a month to collect the supplies, sit and rest, and receive prayers. The farmer started to feel a real change, seeing God in each corner of his town and a revitalization of his church.

Although these positive changes drew more people to the church, they also taxed the already old building and drew heavily on the small congregation's limited volunteer force. The stress began to mount. Finally, after never installing media before, a desire for media of any kind in the 100-year-old sanctuary arose. The farmer thought this upgrade to be the next step after observing the consistent use of smartphones among mothers at the diaper distribution ministry. Other churches used screens, so they should too; but the available resources in the budget were limited, and the short-term fundraising only raised so much. It worked once before, so the pastor asked to access the endowment for these improvements. Soon enough, the slowly building tension erupted into a public conflict.

The first noticeable tension came when volunteers stopped coming to monthly supply distribution events. Some weeks, only the pastor and the retired farmer attended. Things reached a tipping point when rumors of financial mismanagement, selfish kingdom-building aspirations, and poor worship leading began to circulate in the farmer's favorite local coffee shop. The rumors started among some long-time members of the church who did not appreciate the sudden changes. The treasurer stopped providing timely financial reports. This escalated at a monthly congregational meeting when the overseers of the endowment refused to allocate some of their resources to update the sanctuary and other portions of the building, leading to a shouting match. The sudden release of pressure that accumulated over the year caught the pastor off-guard, quickly losing control of the meeting. Members expelled decades worth of past mistakes upon one another. In retrospect, the farmer expected this outcome, but thought the church could handle one more improvement before this strong pushback from them. Ultimately, he overestimated his influence and ability to sustain momentum.

The farmer and the pastor had coffee together at the parsonage, since the farmer did not feel comfortable at the coffee shops he regularly visited. They reviewed material from a conflict management training their church participated in a few years back and decided that they should visit each person in the church, one-on-one, to apologize and listen to their concerns. Some church members received this gesture well, while others felt frustrated about the meeting and stopped attending that church. For three months, the pastor and the farmer made the rounds, visiting people in their homes, businesses, and fields. As the congregants shared their concerns about financial strains, the amount of time these new ministries required from them, and how they did not feel invited into the changes, the tension slowly decreased.

By listening to the people's concerns, the farmer and the pastor began to understand their mistake of moving too quickly and, at times, unilaterally. They did not invite the members into participation, which led to the members to feel as if the church saw them as employees without a say in the development of an organization. The farmer and the pastor did not adequately communicate the spiritual awakening experienced in their own lives with the larger congregation. Listening to the congregation helped the leadership to develop new methods of communication, training, and participation in future ministry opportunities. Their next ministry experiment centered around reading and reflecting on Scripture as a community and listening for the spirit of God together in their church and town.

A young pastor in a neighborhood church collapsed onto her couch after another twelve-hour day. She was pastor of this church for only a year, but it felt like a decade. Every week was filled with hospital visits, late-night multi-hour board meetings, building maintenance decisions, mid-week Bible studies, special worship events, and weekly worship services. Like many congregations, this church came to rely on attractional program-oriented ministries and events that drew heavily on the time, energy, and skills of lay leaders and staff. For several years, these programs and events hallmarked the church's identity, but recently less people volunteered, thus increasing pressure on church staff and the limited number of reliable volunteers. This led the previous pastor, who relocated to a new congregation, to exhaustion.

During the interim period, the church members realized they could no longer keep up with the incredible demands of the church's many programs. The support and excitement of families who joined the church for the programs turned to discouragement. When the new pastor arrived, the congregation impulsively created new programs and attractional events to encourage new people to visit the church. They tried events that worked in the past, like mid-week Bible studies, outdoor movie nights, harvest festivals, and youth concerts. These events found limited success and drained what was left of the volunteers' energy. They felt defeated and exhausted.

As the new pastor reflected on the past year, she knew something had to change to maintain her own sanity and the health of the church and its members. She asked the church members what initially brought them to the church; what about ministry brought them joy; what brought them pain; and which ministries connected the members and which events and ministries pushed them apart. After speaking with church members for a few weeks, she found that many of the members most enjoyed the moments right before and after events where they talked with and spent time with each other.

The pastor reflected on this discovery with a group of fellow pastors during a monthly ministerial alliance lunch. One of the fellow pastors asked what it would look like to create opportunities for people simply to visit with one another. If the conversations before and after events were their favorite part, why not create opportunities for them to do that without the events?

Inspired by the conversation, the pastor introduced opportunities for the church members to visit with each other without the hassle of event planning. For one weekly gathering, she hosted church members in her back yard around a fire pit, a casual opportunity for people to drop in and out in the evening. These "Fire with Friends" gatherings allowed members to visit with one another, share about their week, and enjoy the presence of the fire. Another opportunity took place at a restaurant for mid-morning brunch, where people could drop by for an hour, drink some coffee, and enjoy the presence of others.

After a few months of these gatherings, the pastor introduced intentional conversation topics to the otherwise informal gatherings. She would ask people to share the story of their baptism, explain what initially drew them to the church, who were the most influential people in their spiritual journeys, or a time when they felt God present or absent in their lives. As members shared their stories, they were drawn more deeply into each other's lives and thus regained the joy of serving at the church. People who did not engage in the church's ministries before now attended the more informal gatherings, leading to their engagement in other areas of the church as well. Over time the congregation saw themselves differently. They were no longer the program church; now they are the relational church.

The TSA screening line was backed up farther than normal. As a group of six denominational leaders approached the back of the line, they started to discuss the purpose of this weekend trip out west. They were about to board a two-hour flight to participate in an annual state conference where members from nearly eighty churches would be present. The group of six felt apprehensive. Nobody from their offices had been invited to this conference in three decades. The conference leaders and the congregations that made up the region did not greatly trust the denomination from those years. Nobody remembered how the animosity began. It could have been as simple as personality differences between leaders now long retired. Perhaps a difference of opinion on the most vital ministries caused tension between them. Whatever induced this mistrust, thirty years had passed since any partnership between the region and the denominational body occurred.

A few months prior, the new denominational leader boarded this same flight in an intentional effort to reach out to the leaders of the state region and churches. After a few meals together, they realized they had more in common than they previously thought and felt it was time for the two bodies to explore possible avenues of ministry partnership again. No lofty plans were made, just a simple reintroduction of the two groups. So here they were—six denominational leaders getting on a plane with the hope to reunite two groups who, after a two-hundred-year history of ministry partnership, had ceased contact for decades.

After collecting their luggage and cramming into a small van, the team traveled another two hours through farmland to the church hosting the annual meeting. Along the way, each leader took turns talking about best possible approaches to the upcoming meeting. Nobody really knew what was going to happen. They had a schedule, but not much else.

They knew their first meeting was over dinner that evening, filled with introductions and conversations around banquet tables. Everyone agreed this was a major step and that stakes were high.

A few hours later the six leaders gathered in a classroom in the church. They could see and hear the crowd gather through the partially open door. The also noticed, for the first time, the head table. They had hoped to sit at various tables and meet as many new people as possible. Instead, the state conference planning team created special seats of honor up front for everyone to see.

The denominational leader gathered his team together for a quick word of prayer and encouragement. After the prayer, he looked up and said, "I want each of you to take a turn tonight to tell your testimony. Nothing more. No ministry promotions, no denominational news, no greetings. Just tell your story of how you became a follower of Jesus and were called to this denominational ministry." Everyone looked at each other and mentally and spiritually prepared for the next couple of hours.

As the meal progressed, the state leaders finally introduced the denominational team to the few hundred conference attendees and handed the first person the microphone. Each person on the team took turns telling their story. With each story, the stare of those in attendance softened into faces of acceptance and welcome. With each story, the denominational team realized that despite working together for years, most had never heard each other's stories. By the time the final person shared his story, the denominational team grew closer to each other, and three decades of separation between denomination and region ended.

By sharing their stories, the regional leaders and attendees representing their local churches were reminded of the common ground as followers of Jesus. They all had experienced the saving grace of Christ, were called to a variety of ministerial contexts, and could certainly find ways to partner with each other in corporate mission and ministry. It would take time to work through the years of differences and ministry perspectives, but at least they were now receptive to partnership as fellow followers of Jesus, not adversaries.

The ingredients for her famous homemade cherry pie covered the kitchen island. In just a few hours, a group of people from the church and some friends from next door would be coming over for dinner, Scripture, and storytelling. She could not foresee the upcoming evening, but trusted the pastor who promoted these table groups. Due to her introversion, she found attending big functions and serving in ministry groups with more than a few trusted friends difficult. After a one-on-one talk with the pastor, she finally agreed she would venture out into this unknown territory.

The church formed nine table groups, each consisting of six participants. These table groups gathered for meals in homes for Scripture, prayer, storytelling, and communion. The table groups coordinator helped schedule meeting times and locations. Tonight, it was her turn to host her group of six. Although she had been a member of her church for fifteen years, she could not remember if anybody planning to attend her table group that evening had previously been to her home. As she poured the pie mix into pans she reflected on how odd it seemed to spend every week with a group of people in prayer, study, and ministry for that long and never invite them to your home.

Her neighbor, who moved to the neighborhood with her family to be closer to her church, arrived early to help with the final arrangements. The commonalities of having children close in age, loving a good meal, and sharing similar hobbies allowed the families to quickly develop a friendship. Tonight, she needed help setting up for the table group and wanted the support of a fellow introvert to help play the part of host.

When everyone arrived, they gathered around the table in the dining room with some overflowing into the living room. The meal was a simple but savory soup with a crispy salad and warm bread. The conversation and laughter were genuine and infectious. When the main meal was complete everyone helped clear the table and wash a few dishes. Everyone gathered back at the table and reflected as a group on a short biblical text gaining key insights from everyone in the group, including her eleven-year-old daughter and the sixty-year-old church choir member.

As she brought out her famous cherry pie, two members shared their life stories with the group. Their stories were unique, but similar in many respects. They shared their childhood memories, pains from their young adulthood, faith challenges, struggles and doubts, their moments of celebrations and signs of God's presence in their lives. It was a refreshing change of pace from the brief exchanges they normally shared in church parking lots, grocery stores, and across neighborhood fences. These people poured their hearts out, and she was glad to be part of this group and hoped she had the courage to share as openly when her time came during the next gathering at someone else's home.

The evening concluded with one final symbolic meal around the table. She set out some of the bread from earlier and poured drink into a common chalice. Together as a group they read again the story of Jesus' final meal with his disciples. They passed the bread, dipped into the cup, and prayed together, thanking Christ for his presence at this table and in the lives of those gathered. The rest of the week she walked with a little extra bounce in her step, recognizing Christ's presence in her place of work and in the face of her neighbor who helped set up and clean, and when Sunday morning came around again she and her family went to worship with an enthusiasm they had not experienced in a few months.

Table Life

The preceding stories are all based on actual table life experiences. Stories like these help us wrap our minds around the key spiritual disciplines necessary for living a table life: eating, dwelling in the Word, storytelling, listening, and communion. These disciplines remind us that we cannot grow in Christ alone. We need a community of people who help observe the presence of God in our communities, interpret Scripture, and encourage us to walk boldly in the ways of Jesus.

When younger, my faith tradition heavily emphasized what Dallas Willard called a "gospel of sin management."[7] It emphasized personal Bible studies and daily prayers called "quiet times." Of course, we should all read the Bible daily for information and formation and be in regular communication with God. This is not the problem. The problem is that I was only ever taught these two disciplines. However intentional or unintentional, I was taught that two disciplines fully described the meaning of discipleship in Jesus. Read the Bible and pray, if you do those two things, it will go well with you. If you want to learn more about either of these things, go to church every time the doors were open.

Jesus pointed out the same tendency in the Pharisees in John 5:31ff. He gets to the heart of the matter in John 5:39-40: "You study the Scriptures diligently because you think that in them you have eternal life. These are the very Scriptures that testify about me, yet you refuse to come to me to have life." Jesus reveals that an abundant life cannot be found in religious study alone. Practicing a rigorous life of zealous piety will not fill them with the life they seek. Yet those were the very things elevated and celebrated in my youth.

Over time, Christianity in North America has found its primary concern in how to deal with sin, wrongdoing or wrong-being, and its effects. The popular Christian message of "repent and be saved for heaven" only marginally includes, if included at all, everyday life—our actual existence. When we examine the broad spectrum of Christian proclamation and practice, we see that the essential move in conservative theology is forgiving the sins of an individual, while more liberal theology seeks to remove systemic evils. The gospel is then limited to a "gospel of sin management."[8] Under this type of gospel presentation, the message of redemption loses the importance of life and character transformation.

The exclusive practice of this "gospel of sin management" is flawed because it leads to forms of fundamentalism, no matter one's theological or political ideology, hinging on the belief that what we do is more important than who we are. This goes directly against the gospel message that proclaims God's love for us, in spite of our actions, whether good or bad. Sometimes we need a reminder that we are beloved people made in the image of God and that knowing that this is our primary identity holds significant weight as an important truth. Our calling as Christians is to pursue a deeper awareness of Christ's presence in our lives and the world he created. We must learn to trust in God's personal care and love for us as individuals and as a whole. We must pursue love of God and others just as Jesus taught. This requires us to acknowledge that God loves all of his creation, and this includes everyone. When we understand our identity as beloved by God we will want to respond with appropriate actions like praying, reading Scripture, evangelism, and faithful obedience to the teachings of Christ. But those actions are not where our identity rest; they are an extension of our identity as children made in the image of the Creator.

The "gospel of sin management" paradigm I inherited as a youth also believes that the pursuit of Christ is possible without community. Scripture reading, prayer, evangelism, penance, and moral behavior can be practiced without larger community connections to the spiritual body in any way, but can they be done well? Of course not. The extreme individualism of the "gospel of sin management" fails to engage faithfully with the everyday, ordinary elements of life and does not acknowledge the need for life-giving community. Seeking to be your own spiritual guide and moral thermometer is a form of idolatry, and it will ultimately leave you morally, emotionally, and spiritually bankrupt.

Ultimately, the "gospel of sin management" misses "a coherent framework of knowledge and practical direction adequate to personal formation toward the abundance and obedience emphasized in the New Testament, with a corresponding redemption of ordinary life" along with the affirmation of journeying with others.[9] Thus "the gospel of sin management" only converses with "the other" to use them as examples of model behavior or wickedness or as target groups for evangelism.

In reality, we share the church and the world with men and women who have experienced powerful encounters with Christ. We need their wisdom and insights to guide us through difficult terrain. Like mountain Sherpas guiding climbers to a summit, they have already been to the top and know the way. We need their wisdom to keep us from pursuing routes that will only lead us off the mountain. Although sometimes difficult, we need to listen to the perspective of others and learn from their hard-earned insights.

A full community experience includes participating in another person's struggle with what it means to be a follower of

Christ. Sometimes, people seriously doubt and question life and holiness. People may find opening a Bible, praying, or attending church regularly difficult. People may be disenfranchised, abused, and mistreated without anyone to listen. We need their questions, skepticism, and perspective to remind us that sometimes following Jesus can feel trying, unnatural, or inapplicable to a certain context.

Personal piety may seem appealing due to its neatness. You need only worry about your personal faith journey and moral struggles. You are not accountable or responsible to anyone except yourself. When we notice our ethical behaviors and thoughts have drifted away from our individual pursuit of righteousness, we can apply an appropriate amount of guilt until we create a new regimen of actions that help get it back on track.

This type of approach to personal and spiritual maturity will always leave you stunted and underdeveloped. The mirror is rarely a good litmus test. A deep look in the mirror may encourage or perhaps startle you, but it cannot change your reflection. We are not designed for long-term solitary approaches to life or matters of faith. Seasons of personal reflection and introspection are good and healthy, but the most successful ventures are conducted in a community context. For additional help we might consider working under the guidance of an individual like a spiritual director, therapist, or counselor. These gifted members of the church can supplement and give clarity to the community experience without replacing our engagement with the larger community. Spiritual maturation in Christ means becoming more comfortable with the messiness of sharing our space, faith, thoughts, and experience with others.

The Church at a Crossroads

The North American church is at a significant crossroads. Author, speaker, and ordained pastor Skye Jethani observed in an online article for *Premier Christianity* that each time the world experiences a sudden technological advancement the church is deeply affected.[10] The Roman Road network of the first century allowed the transmission of letters to various churches in the empire and created the foundation for our New Testament. The creation of the printing press allowed the Bible and other content to reach more people than previously possible. The rapid spread of ideas helped to spark the Protestant Reformation and shifted the focus of the worship experience from the Eucharist toward preaching. Jethani notes that when the Bible became more accessible the importance of accurate interpretation increased. Therefore, preaching and teaching the Bible took center stage in the worship experience. The demand for quality Christian teaching heightened, while the amount of available teachers decreased.

Presently, we are in the midst of incredible technological advancements. We have access to more information on more devices than ever before. Church leaders, pastors, authors, and other creators of Christian content utilize podcasts, live streaming videos, blog posts, websites, and various other media to their full potential. Christians no longer receive all their teaching, preaching, and church content from their local church's preaching pastor's thirty-minute monologue. We have also entered an age when more and more people identify less and less with the institutional church. Many look for new outlets and points of connection with other Christians. As a result, we have entered an age when the amount of content has outstripped the demand.

Well-planned and -led Christ-centered worship services reorient our hearts, minds, and souls to become more in tune with the Father, Son, and Holy Spirit. This allows us to live out our calling as active participants in the kingdom of God. Churches can provide quality preaching and teaching as part of the weekly worship experience. But we must not mistake Christian content in its various formats for the Christian experience in the local church. There is plenty of content to go around, and much of it is of higher quality than the average local church can provide. We must ask ourselves, what is the purpose of the local church if not to share Christian content? Now might be time to reorient how we spend our church gathering times and rethink how to be the local church.

The local church and local pastors spend countless ministry hours and financial resources each week preparing and creating intense media-driven speaking times. What if we considered using that same amount of time and financial resources being with people in our community and practicing spiritual disciplines like table life during the week? Rather than competing with the massive amounts of available content, what if the local church pastor and leaders *curated* the best and most contextually vital content available through new media technology for the people of the local church? What would it look like if the local church focused more on providing community elements of the Christian experience, such as table fellowship and communion, which cannot be easily accessed in other ways? What things can we only do as a gathered community and what things can be done with other formats?[11]

Table life fosters discipleship habits that draw people closer to God, to one another, and to the local church. Table life brings people together around a meal to practice spiritual disciplines that bring fullness to life. Eating with others is the catalyst that makes other things possible. Gathering around the table is a sacred event; it creates space for the Spirit to move. Meals create an environment where conversations happen. The table births and deepens relationships. The table is where fundamentally human events take place. A table life actively seeks, welcomes, and celebrates the presence of Christ within those events.

Table life habits of discipleship easily extend into the places we live, work, and play. Neighborhood connections are made and strengthened by inviting neighbors to the table. Our digital lives and social media encounters are elevated when shaped by the community-building disciplines of table life. All the places we live provide the context for which the hope of Jesus is applied.

Living a table life cultivates a series of habits that create a holistic approach that helps you become more aware of the presence of Christ in your life and the lives of those around you. The intentional habits of eating together, dwelling in the word, listening, storytelling, and communion create space for the Holy Spirit to work in yourself and in the community gathered around the table. When these disciplines are practiced in the context of a church, communities are drawn closer to one another as they are drawn closer to Christ.

Table life is simple in its concept, but it is not simplistic in its application. Table life will not provide quick results; however, it will garner lasting results. Like any spiritual discipline, table life requires you to create space in your life for related practices. It can be tempting to stop hosting or attending meals. It is not always comfortable or practical to have multiple guests in your home. It is sometimes easier to skip out on an invitation or evade an online meeting than to rearrange your schedule. Sometimes we seek to talk more than listen and that makes knowing how God acts in the lives of other harder. Other times we seek to keep our narratives to ourselves, which prevents us from meaningful self-reflection and deprives those close to you of learning how God works in your life. It might be tempting to skip communion due to feelings of intimidation or perhaps awkwardness if you do not have much experience leading communion, but the benefits of these habits are deep. Those who regularly exercise the habits of eating with others, Scripture reading, listening, storytelling, and communion will be more capable of recognizing Christ in every aspect of their life. Exercising these habits helps develop you into a person who builds up community. Engaging in spiritual habits like these prepares you to share what Christ has done and continues to do in your life and in the life of your community.

Conclusion

Living a table life helps us to learn and experience habits of discipleship that connect people to Christ, the church, and one another in powerful ways. It connects rich spiritual disciplines with the everyday stuff of life, directly combating the temptation to focus on a "gospel of sin management" or burn out on shallow social engagement. The habits of eating together, dwelling in the Word, listening, storytelling, and communion provide participants with space to embody teachings about the kingdom of God in a variety of contexts and strengthen their relationships with others.

It's time to pull up a chair and start living a table life.

NOTES

1. Alan J. Roxburgh, *Joining God, Remaking Church, Changing the World: The New Shape of the Church in Our Time* (New York: Morehouse, 2015), 60–62.
2. Simon Carey Holt, *Eating Heaven: Spirituality at the Table* (Brunswick, Australia: Acorn Press, 2013), sec. 107.
3. Holt, *Eating Heaven* sec. 107.
4. For the effect of these changes on the church, see "The Church at a Crossroads," pages 17–19.
5. Eugene H. Peterson, *Five Smooth Stones for Pastoral Work* (Grand Rapids, MI: Eerdmans, 1992), 2.
6. Holt, *Eating Heaven*, sec. 131.

7. Dallas Willard, *The Divine Conspiracy: Rediscovering Our Hidden Life in God*, 1st ed. (San Francisco: Harper San Francisco, 1998), 41.

8. Ibid.

9. Ibid.

10. Skye Jethani, "The case against sermon-centric Sundays," *Premier Christianity*, https://www.premierchristianity.com/Past-Issues/2019/October-2019/The-case-against-sermon-centric-Sundays.

11. Due to the unique COVID-19 pandemic of 2020, churches across the world continue to be forced to answer these sorts of questions in new ways.

2

How Meals Shape Us

The summer before third grade was the first time I remember walking into a church fellowship hall. I remember being impressed by the size of the space. High ceilings, big walls, a stage, and a few basketball hoops filled the outer edges of the room. In the middle stood countless round tables set with disposable cutlery, napkins, and the standard-issue red plastic cups that were so popular in the 1990s. A set of eight slightly rusted cold metal folding chairs surrounded each table. Against one wall sat a set of long tables pushed together to create a buffet line. Each table bowed in the middle with age and the weight of mismatched slow cookers, casserole dishes, baking pans, chicken boxes, and other containers overflowing with food and desserts. There must have been a hundred adults milling about on the tile floor talking, directing traffic, and wrangling the noisy children. The cacophony of voices, smells, and sights was brought to instant silence when an elderly woman asked the pastor to pray over the dinner through a static-filled PA system. After everyone unanimously droned an "Amen," the noise returned as everyone lined up at the warped table to pile food on their plates. As my mother, sister, and I sat down at one of the tables after getting food, I felt a little awkward as people we did not know introduced themselves, asked how old my sister and I were, and if our family was new to the neighborhood. I was eight, my sister was six, and we had just moved. I don't remember much else about the day except leaving that fellowship hall knowing something important just happened. I left feeling very full and very loved. I remember feeling like I was part of something special. I also remember feeling a little confused as to why they kept their basketball hoops in the same room where they ate dinner; my mom never let me bring toys to the table at home.

The Function of Meals

FOSTERING COMMUNITY

Meals foster community in profound ways. The act of sharing a table with another person prepares us to genuinely see others and be seen by them in return. The habit of gathering around the table allows us to see people as "the image of God, connecting us to that uniquely precious person, and giving them the space and security they need to reveal their authentic self. The hosts also leave themselves vulnerable enough to reveal their own authentic selves . . . [s]haring a meal with someone is one of the most intimate things we can do."[1] Eating meals with another is a form of holy presence that has diminished in our modern world, even among Christians.

> Daily, we obsess about holding our lives together. We walk in isolation and protection from other people. We pass homeless people on the street and give a dollar, but we do not know them. Indeed, we dare not know them. At work we look at clients as profit-loss statements. Even our most intimate relationships can turn into negotiated contracts. As a result there's a distrustful distance between people in

> all types of relationships. We are empty and long for some kind—any kind—of presence.[2]

Eating meals with others creates the holy space necessary for meaningful relationships to develop. Without some sort of intentional practice to form habits of faithful presence to God and other people, we will continue to feel the "emptiness that creeps back in, alerting us that there is something missing."[3]

CREATING A FAMILY IDENTITY

Jesus taught that the sum of the Scriptures and the human experience is to love God and to love others. He exhibited this love through sharing meals with others, reflecting on Scripture, listening, and storytelling. These mealtime habits created new family identities as Jesus encourages his tablemates to see their fellow diners as brothers and sisters. The apostle Paul also frequently uses the word *adelphoi* ("brothers and sisters") to refer to Christians within the church community, demonstrating his concern with its interpersonal workings.[4] Following the teachings of Jesus, Paul wants the church community to relate to one another as family.

The earliest Christians exhibited habits distinctive from, and intriguing to, the cultures around them. When challenged about their ideas and beliefs, the earliest Christians pointed to their familial behavior as an enactment of their beliefs.[5] Our modern western culture is more individualistic than the first-century Mediterranean world. This current individualism has resulted in a tendency to undervalue the communal identity of Christian theology and praxis that were so important to Jesus and the New Testament authors.

> The story of the Bible is not simply about the salvation of individuals. The story of the Bible is about the creation of

> one faithful, saved people of God, Israel. That story for Christians means the expansion of that one people of God to include Gentiles, for what God is doing in this world is creating one universal people. Paul's mission [and that of the church] is about expanding God's people by including Gentiles into the one people of God, the church.[6]

The church is where we learn to become "one universal people" shaped by the symbols of bread and cup. Full meals in homes, church potlucks, chats in coffee shops, and even snacks in the church nursery cultivate the necessary habits within a church community that bring the members closer to becoming the family of God. The culture of the United States highly values the individual while diminishing the concept of community. "We primarily speak of a 'personal relationship with God' as the fundamental goal of faith. There is nothing wrong with personal faith, but the love that Jesus speaks of is fundamentally other-oriented and generally communal. If the goal of church is self, we will not fulfill Jesus' command that we be known as a people of love."[7]

The communal, other-oriented nature of the church emerges in the writings of the New Testament. The pronoun "you" primarily appears as plural. When we read the epistles and pastoral letters in the New Testament and come across the word *you* it might do us well to default to reading it as "you all." So, when one reads "you are the light of the world" in Matthew 5:14; "you yourselves are God's temple and that God's Spirit dwells in your midst" in 1 Corinthians 3:16; "offer your bodies as living sacrifices" and "have your minds renewed" in Romans 12:1-2; receiving Jesus Christ as Lord and living in him in Colossians 2:6; or "by grace you have been saved" in Ephesians 2:8, remember that these and thousands of other examples are communal truths. These truths are for both the community and the individual. The church—you all—is communally called into grace and faithful obedience to the ways of Jesus.

PRACTICING HABITS OF DISCIPLESHIP

To build stronger communities we must practice habits of discipleship that foster stronger communities. Alan Kreider teaches that habits are "formed by repetition, by sheer physicality of doing things over and over so that they become habitual, reflexive, and borne in our bodies."[8] James K. A. Smith further elaborates on habit-forming practices when he states, "*Habitus* is acquired, is learned, by incarnate pedagogies that in oblique, allusive, cunning ways work on the body and thus orient the whole person."[9] Learning to treat fellow Christians as brothers and sisters in Christ as a regular habit requires followers of Jesus to eat together, read Scripture together, share stories, and participate in communion. When practiced often, mirroring the mealtime habits of Jesus and treating fellow believers as brothers and sisters become more natural. Those who participate in such habits start to learn and physically embody how to be present with God and their fellow diners.

FOLLOWING THE EXAMPLE OF JESUS

English pastor and author Tim Chester asks, "How would you complete this sentence: 'The Son of Man came . . . ?'"[10] Many of us might state that the Son of Man came to forgive sins, preach and teach, or embody the kingdom of God. While each of these statements would be true in themselves, the New Testament completes the sentence in three ways: "the Son of Man came not to be served but to serve, and to give his life as a ransom for many" (Mark 10:45, ESV); "the Son of Man came to seek and to save the lost" (Luke 19:10); "The Son of Man came eating and drinking" (Luke 7:34).

The first two familiar verses tell us why Jesus came. He came to serve, to give his life as a ransom, to seek and to save those created in the image of God. But how did Jesus accomplish these purposes? If the first two verses tell us why Jesus came as the incarnate presence of God, the third verse gives us the method. Jesus came eating and drinking.[11] Jesus was such a notorious diner and imbiber that the crowds around Jesus created a saying about him: "Here is a glutton and a drunkard, a friend of tax collectors and sinners" (Luke 7:34).

Meals were such a significant part of how Jesus went about his mission that of all the symbolic acts Jesus could have given his followers that encompassed his identity, teaching, and mission, he chose a meal. New Testament scholar Robert J. Karris is known for saying that "Jesus is either going to a meal, at a meal, or coming from a meal."[12] Jesus eats with fishermen, tax collectors, Zealots, men and women, sick people, religious leaders, outcasts, tourists, sinners, Gentiles, Jews, and many others. Jesus spends his final night with his closest friends around a meal, identifying his own body as bread and his blood as drink. People and meals are so important to Jesus that he told his closest followers to remember him each time they gathered to eat (Luke 22:19).

Meal Traditions in Biblical Times

Jesus carried forward the great biblical tradition of meals serving as ways to embody covenant and community. Eating inappropriately, however, can be a sign of division and selfishness. Both are seen in Scripture. The Bible begins with a garden full of food and fellowship. A meal wrongly eaten breaks covenant and began the redemption story of God's faithful presence. Jacob stole a bowl of soup for a birthright; Abraham made a meal for angelic messengers; Joseph revealed his identity to his brothers over lunch; Israel was given manna from heaven in the wilderness; Gideon was found hiding in a winepress to protect his culinary resources; and Elijah and a widow survived on a miraculous supply of oil and flour.

Bread, lamb, herbs, and wine mark time and God's salvation work through the Passover and Exodus.

The biblical meal tradition continued into the eighth and sixth centuries BCE, when the people of Israel experienced a painful and devastating series of exiles. During this period, the prophets presented the people of Israel with their sinful culpability that led to exile. They also cast a vision of hopeful restoration and salvation that included a messianic banquet, a great feast where the Lord will serve as the host and healer. This hoped-for feast would be a place where Israel and the nations could gather and have their spiritual and physical needs met in full. The most important passage outlining this hope is Isaiah 25:6-9:

> On this mountain the Lord Almighty will prepare
> a feast of rich food for all peoples,
> a banquet of aged wine—
> the best of meats and the finest of wines.
> On this mountain he will destroy
> the shroud that enfolds all peoples,
> the sheet that covers all nations;
> he will swallow up death forever.
> The Sovereign Lord will wipe away the tears
> from all faces;
> he will remove his people's disgrace
> from all the earth.
> The Lord has spoken.
>
> In that day they will say,
>
> "Surely this is our God;
> we trusted in him, and he saved us.
> This is the Lord, we trusted in him;
> let us rejoice and be glad in his salvation."

This passage speaks of a hope that one day God alone will rule from a high mountain in Jerusalem, where an elaborate meal with the best foods and wine will be available. This heavenly banquet offers hope for all creation, inviting the nations to God's table. Those gathered celebrate the work of the king, who has won a great victory and removed the effects of the garden dwellers' choice to determine for themselves the difference between good and evil by eating wrongly. At this messianic banquet, the death that has ruled the earth since the time of Adam and Eve is defeated, and the shroud that has covered the nations in disgrace is removed. The people who are present at the banquet will respond in praise of the Host who has made this possible.

THE ANCIENT MEDITERRANEAN WORLD

In the centuries following the exile, a series of successive empires would conquer the land of Israel, each leaving cultural and culinary marks. To remain authentic to their own culture amidst the rule of the empire, the Jewish people strengthened their kosher customs but were still being influenced by the cultures around them. Formal meals in the ancient Mediterranean world were a common reality. "If we are to understand properly any individualized instance of formalized meals in the Greco-Roman world, such as Greek philosophical banquets, or Jewish festival meals, or early Christian community meals, we must first understand the larger phenomenon of the banquet as a social institution."[13]

Greek and Roman banquet meals, like the Jewish kosher and festival meals, were a means of creating and solidifying social bonds and hierarchies.[14] "Because of the clear boundary-defining symbolism of table fellowship in the ancient world, banquets became a significant feature of various identifiable social groups. The social code of the banquet represents a confirmation and ritualization of the boundaries that exist in a social situation."[15] By emphasizing social order around the banquet table, participants proclaimed the social order of the world around them and their place in it. However, by the first century, these formal meals had degenerated so far into gluttony and drunkenness that contemporary writers satirized them.[16]

During such events, guests would sit by social rank and honor. The host sat at one end of the room with the most important guests to his right in descending order around the room. In a Roman banquet, three couches stood against the outer perimeter of the room, with food presented to the guests on low tables in front of them, from which they would have helped themselves with their hands. This seating arrangement became known as a *triclinium* for its U-shaped table containing three sides. Slaves brought in the food and attended to everyone's needs. Gender roles and class distinctions were clearly defined. After the meal, raucous entertainment or political conversation would follow.[17]

The impact of these feasts was so deep that by the first century it became common for families to sit in banquet style even when lacking the ability to adhere to the opulence of banquet. In poorer settings, bread, salt, and water made up much of the meal, supplemented with cheese or other local foods; sometimes leftovers from a wealthier banquet might be included. Not having the luxury of special couches, participants would sit on cushions on the ground.[18] Such formal meals created and strengthened social bonds between participants while also defining boundaries between communities and reinforcing status within them.[19]

FIRST-CENTURY JEWISH PRACTICES

Jewish feasts gradually adopted some of the Greco-Roman conquerors' banquet etiquette.[20] The starkest difference would have been the dietary restrictions, which led Jews to hold banquets and meals unto themselves, limiting their dining with Gentiles. However, some compromise was inevitable, especially for those living outside the boundaries of Israel. The need to be able to survive and do business outside of Israel required accommodation.[21]

By participating in these unique mealtime traditions, the Jewish people participated in an act of nonviolent cultural rebellion that served as a sign of God's kingdom. It created a different rhythm from the world around them. Every kosher meal, festival feast, and period of fasting served as reminders that they were a counter-cultural witness as people of God.

By the first century, communal meals served as acts of social acceptance and religious fellowship. Eating was theology. For the first-century Jew and Gentile alike, dining created an intimate setting where relationships were nurtured among like-minded people. It was a fundamental belief that to share your table with someone deemed unworthy by social or religious standards would corrupt you and make you unholy. Like a communicable virus, social and religious impurity was thought to be contagious.[22] To share a meal with someone was an act of applied theology that affirmed God's love and acceptance of another.

This is what got Jesus into so much trouble with the social and religious gatekeepers. Their grievance with Jesus was not that he ate with the wrong sorts of people, but that he would eat with anybody. Norman Perrin describes Jesus' table habits like this:

> Normally, a table's prime function is to establish social ranking and hierarchy (by what one eats, how one eats, with whom one eats). Normally, a meal is about social identification, status and power . . . But the very randomness of Jesus' table habits challenged this system of social relations modeled on meals and manners . . . it was not

> simply that Jesus ate with objectionable persons—outcasts and sinners—but that he ate with anyone, indiscriminately! . . . The table companionship practiced by Jesus thus recreated the world, redrew all of society's maps and flow charts. Instead of symbolizing social rank and order, it blurred the distinctions between hosts and guests, need and plenty. Instead of reinforcing rules of etiquette, it subverted them, making the last first and the first last.[23]

Eating exclusively with his disciples and religious leaders would have secured Jesus' social status as a pious rabbi. If he stayed at common tables with fishermen, farmers, and carpenters, people would have known him as a day laborer and thus his station in life. If Jesus supped with tax collectors, Roman soldiers, and civic leaders, people could have identified him as a swindler who ate from the tables of those who extorted righteous Jews. If Jesus foraged for scraps and leftovers with prostitutes, beggars, and the infirm, people would have branded him a sinner, insulted him, and overlooked him according to proper social order. However, Jesus' ability to move between groups confused the culture.

The Gospels are replete with examples of Jesus refusing to feed into the social hierarchies that banquets and symposiums reinforced. His ability to interact with all sorts of people created space for any day to include a simple breakfast with his disciples, a bread-and-fish lunch on a hillside with thousands of ethnically mixed people of various religious affiliation, and a banquet feast dinner at the home of a Pharisee where a prostitute might break in and seek absolution. In a world where community was defined by social hierarchy, meals with Jesus created new families shaped by holiness.

Jesus' Practices of Table Fellowship

CONCENTRIC CIRCLES OF TABLE FELLOWSHIP

Mark 3 serves as an example of how Jesus goes through a progression of relationships where he provides new identities to those who gather around his table. In just a few verses Jesus heals sick people from a large crowd, identifies his disciples, debates with religious leaders, and creates a new family in God.

> Jesus withdrew with his disciples to the lake, and a large crowd from Galilee followed. When they heard about all he was doing, many people came to him from Judea, Jerusalem, Idumea, and the regions across the Jordan and around Tyre and Sidon. Because of the crowd he told his disciples to have a small boat ready for him, to keep the people from crowding him. For he had healed many, so that those with diseases were pushing forward to touch him. Whenever the impure spirits saw him, they fell down before him and cried out, "You are the Son of God." But he gave them strict orders not to tell others about him. (Mark 3:7-12)

As Jesus journeys through the region of Galilee his popularity precedes him, causing large crowds to form. People from Galilee, Judea, Jerusalem, Idumea, and areas east of the Jordon River like Tyre and Sidon all gather to meet Jesus. These are all places connected to the borders of Israel when David was king. This fact helps to connect Jesus' story to Israel's story of the promised messiah from the line of David. These places are also a reflection of the multicultural context that made up Israel. Because Israel in general, and Galilee in particular, was a significant travel center filled with trade routes, it is important to remember that any broad crowd would have potentially encompassed people from multiple ethnic and religious backgrounds. Within these crowds there would have been both Gentiles who ate broadly and used hierarchy to establish table fellowship and faithful Jews shaped by the Torah, exercising narrow eating habits, and observing the multiple annual holy feasts.

Jesus responds to their presence by healing their sick, casting out demons, and telling them the kingdom of God has come near, with all the political and religious implications that such a proclamation carries. Jesus demonstrates the possibility of Isaiah 25 on a Galilean hillside, showing the nations together for a meal, their needs met, and their sick healed. Only the demons seem to comprehend the gravity of this scene as they cry out, "You are the Son of God" upon seeing him.

> Jesus went up on a mountainside and called to him those he wanted, and they came to him. He appointed twelve that they might be with him and that he might send them out to preach and to have authority to drive out demons. These are the twelve he appointed: Simon (to whom he gave the name Peter), James son of Zebedee and his brother John (to them he gave the name Boanerges, which means "sons of thunder"), Andrew, Philip, Bartholomew, Matthew, Thomas, James son of Alphaeus, Thaddaeus, Simon the Zealot and Judas Iscariot, who betrayed him. (Mark 3:13-19)

Jesus pulls away from the crowds to climb a mountain overlooking the Sea of Galilee. Here he identifies twelve individuals from the crowd who will become his intimate disciples. He commissions them to serve as extensions of his ministry, giving them the power to cast out demons and the confidence to preach. But the most important thing this passage tells us is that these disciples are called to be *with* Jesus: "He appointed the twelve that they might be with him." They are to be with Jesus and witness his ministry in a way the crowds do not. They will be with Jesus when he heals people, feeds the multitudes, walks on water, raises the dead to life, eats his final meal, prays at Gethsemane, and is arrested. These disciples are called to be with the people that Jesus is with, including the crowds, religious leaders, the sick, the demon-possessed, children, the poor, the elite, and everyone in between. These twelve must learn quickly the difference between hanging out with Jesus and being with Jesus. To be with Jesus means they will share in feasts, wedding parties, and healing moments. But they will also share in the toil and grind of ministry, experience the harassment of others, and for ten of them, experience persecution to the point of death.

> Then Jesus entered a house, and again a crowd gathered, so that he and his disciples were not even able to eat. When his family heard about this, they went to take charge of him, for they said, "He is out of his mind."
>
> And the teachers of the law who came down from Jerusalem said, "He is possessed by Beelzebul! By the prince of demons he is driving out demons."
>
> So Jesus called them over to him and began to speak to them in parables: "How can Satan drive out Satan? If a kingdom is divided against itself, that kingdom cannot stand. If a house is divided against itself, that house cannot stand. And if Satan opposes himself and is divided, he cannot stand; his end has come. In fact, no one can enter a strong man's house without first tying him up. Then he can plunder the strong man's house. Truly I tell you, people can be forgiven all their sins and every slander they utter, but whoever blasphemes against the Holy Spirit will never be forgiven; they are guilty of an eternal sin."
>
> He said this because they were saying, "He has an impure spirit."

> Then Jesus' mother and brothers arrived. Standing outside, they sent someone in to call him. A crowd was sitting around him, and they told him, "Your mother and brothers are outside looking for you."
>
> "Who are my mother and my brothers?" he asked.
>
> Then he looked at those seated in a circle around him and said, "Here are my mother and my brothers! Whoever does God's will is my brother and sister and mother." (Mark 3:20-35)

This excerpt introduces two groups simultaneously: Jesus' family and the crowd of people.[24] First, Jesus' family appears quite concerned about his well-being and travel to collect him from the surrounding crowd. Jesus' family realizes that if Jesus continues to heal, teach, and preach to the crowds and commissioning disciples, he is taking important steps toward shaking up the established social order. His family sees the inevitable social backlash to such behavior and want a word with him.

Next, Jesus sits at a dinner table surrounded by people to the point he and his disciples are unable to eat. Teachers of the law, perhaps seeing Jesus in their travels, yell over the crowd and accuse Jesus of consorting with demons. Imagine the room. It is a small, one- or two-room house filled to the rafters with the host family, disciples, religious leaders, and a crowd that most likely consists of people from a variety of backgrounds. Jesus summons them closer to share his teachings. As they approach Jesus, it becomes impossible for them not to touch. Clean and unclean collide as their eyes and ears are collectively fixed on Jesus. He tells a parable that quickly debunks the accusations of the teachers of the law. He then warns them to be careful not to blaspheme against the working of the Spirit.

It is all too easy to throw the teachers of the law under the proverbial bus. We say they are short-sighted and that they miss the kingdom for the laws. They are too worried about croutons and not worried enough about the cripple. Yet, if we are honest with ourselves, we have all taken turns at playing the teacher of the law. After years of indoctrination, study, and personal experience we feel we know the way things should be. We know all the traditions and what they mean. We know who belongs and who needs redemption. We haven't missed a Sunday sermon in years, and we don't require email reminders in our inboxes to know what time the service starts. We know the order of worship without needing a bulletin. We know every year there will be an Easter cantata, a summer VBS, and an annual picnic. We volunteer at the food bank, collect coats for the homeless, host the community Thanksgiving service, and walk through the Sundays of Advent culminating in a Christmas Eve service where we all sing "Away in a Manger" in the dim glow of candlelight. We do this and many other things year in and year out. Not a single detail in this rhythm needs to be altered. We have been doing it long enough to know how best to do them, and anyone who seeks to change the way things are done will quickly learn who is actually in charge of your congregation.

It is easy to poke fun at ourselves. I love every one of those things. I love the rhythm of the church calendar, well-organized worship, local missions, and candlelit services. But it is my suspicion that we often become so focused on the important business of building up our institutions that we have lost the ability to respond to the movement of the Holy Spirit. We have become experts in dealing with perishable goods we call traditions, rites, and rules. When they start to smell of moldy rot, we discard them only to run to the store and replace them with something else that will spoil later.

If Jesus poked around our churches, para-church ministries, and personal ministries, gently guiding us to see the world differently, would we respond by saying, "Yes, I will go" or by telling him he was an agent of Beelzebub?

As Jesus finishes his parable, his family reappears and summons their wayward eldest son out of the house. Jesus' family sees him rocking the societal boat, and they come to collect him and set him straight. Jesus responds to their request for a family meeting by looking around the room filled with crowds, religious leaders, and disciples all gathered around a dinner table and gives them new identities. "Then he looked at those seated in a circle around him and said, 'Here are my mother and my brothers! Whoever does God's will is my brother and sister and mother'" (Mark 3:34-35).

Those who gather around the tables where Jesus is present are brothers and sisters in Christ. The crowds, the disciples, the religious leaders, his family, and the host family are all brothers and sisters together if they follow the will of God. That is the transformative shift that happens around a table where Jesus is the host! When we gather around the table and welcome Jesus as host, we gain new identities. We are no longer limited to being members of a nameless, faceless crowd or institutional preservationists. We are more than students of biblical instruction. We are family members with all who would call on the name of Jesus. We are no longer separated by potential impurity, but instead united in our mutual holiness provided by Jesus.

LOOKING FOR JESUS AROUND THE TABLE

The strong connection between meals and Jesus' identity and character appear in how the disciples recognize Jesus after his resurrection. We will discuss Luke 24:13-35 in detail later, but for now it is sufficient to state that the two despondent followers of Jesus journeying to Emmaus, who did not recognize the presence of Jesus, truly saw him once he took, blessed, broke, and gave the bread around the dinner table. When their eyes were finally opened, they immediately traveled back to Jerusalem and explained their encounter with Jesus by emphasizing "how Jesus was recognized by them when he broke the bread" (Luke 24:35).

In Luke 24:36-44 Jesus again makes his presence known. He appears to the group gathered to hear the Emmaus travelers' story. He greets them with the blessing, "Peace be with you" (Luke 24:36). Initially, out of sheer joy and amazement, the group thinks Jesus is a ghost. Jesus tries to reveal himself physically by asking them to examine his pierced hands, feet, and side. Even this revelation causes them to sink further into a state of excited disbelief. Jesus asks them, "Do you have anything here to eat?" (Luke 26:41), and only after eating a piece of broiled fish and revealing the Scriptures to them do their hearts calm enough to believe and recognize Jesus.

In John 21:1-19, a small group of disciples attempt to regain a sense of normalcy after the crucifixion and resurrection of Jesus by fishing. In John's account, Jesus has already appeared to all the disciples, except Thomas, the first time, and with the entire group a second time. Now we find a group of seven disciples fishing on the Sea of Galilee. They fish all night without much success. Jesus calls out, encouraging them to cast their nets on the other side of the boat, and they bring in a bountiful harvest. Peter recognizes Jesus, who promptly jumps into the lake to swim to shore, allowing his fellow fisherman to bring in the night's miraculous catch. As the disciples approach the shore, Jesus cooks fish and bread for their breakfast. Jesus then asks them to contribute their catch to the food he has already provided. Then, as they sit in a group, Jesus makes eye contact with Peter. While they eat their breakfast as friends and adopted heirs in the kingdom of God, Jesus asks Peter if he loves him three times right in front of everyone. Peter proclaims his love, and Jesus commissions him. It was over a meal that Peter is reconciled both to Jesus and to his fellow disciples.

The tradition of regularly gathering around tables continued into the early church. Each week, people would meet and share full meals in a host home. Just as with Jesus, these meals broke the boundaries of their cultural norms. Roman soldiers shared grapes with Jewish women. Businessmen shared pita and hummus with the homeless person next to them. Gentile civic leaders passed cups of wine to Jewish religious experts. Slaves shared meat with masons. "So in Christ Jesus you are all children of God through faith, for all of you who were baptized into Christ have clothed yourselves with Christ. There is neither Jew nor Gentile, neither slave nor free, nor is there male or female, for you are all one in Christ Jesus" (Galatians 3:26-28). At these meals people ate together, shared their lives, and remembered the story of Jesus. When everyone was full, they sang songs of praise and prayed together.[25]

With a diverse group of attendees, conflict sometimes arose during these meals. Many writings in the New Testament reveal how difficult it was to live in a world re-created by Jesus' resurrection. People ate more than their share without leaving enough for others (1 Corinthians 11). Slaves were not fully welcomed into the community as equals (Philemon). Favoritism for certain members over others reinforced social disparities in need of healing (James 2). Jews and Gentiles argued about the sort of foods most appropriate for personal and corporate consumption (1 Corinthians 8). The whole community, at times, needed a reminder about their call to love one another, to see one another as brothers and sisters (1 Thessalonians 1–4), and of the future banquet feast in heaven (Revelation 21–22).

In short, eating together was both beautiful and messy then and remains so today. Sacrificial meals unite us together as followers of Jesus, redeeming and restoring us. However, when done selfishly, meals can create division and cut deep wounds that may take generations to heal. When we gather around the table and recognize Jesus in our midst, we are part of the feast where Jesus looks around the table and says, "Here are my brothers and sisters and mothers." When we recognize Jesus in a place as ordinary as the dinner table, we realize, like the Emmaus travelers, Peter and the disciples, and Paul and the early church Jesus' continuous presence in all the other ordinary places of our lives. But when we use the table as a place of intentional division and exclusion, we miss what Jesus created for us and will provide for us in the new heaven and new earth.

Practicing Table Fellowship in the Home

My mother always insisted our family eat at a table. No matter where we lived, apartment or house, she always managed to find a table to fit. Our tables ranged from things as simple as a moving box turned upside down to hold a takeout pizza to large tables capable of holding holiday feasts that took days to prepare. I remember a time in late elementary school where we ate in a small kitchen around a table so small everyone's plates touched. I remember times when our table was covered in school projects or debris from the week, and we would have to eat on a blanket on the living room floor. Most meals were simply and lovingly prepared. The point was clear though: we eat together, we face each other, we share our meals and our lives together. These moments left a powerful impact on me. Today my family of four continues this tradition. My family has gone through similar progressions of tabletops made of boxes, sheets of plywood or borrowed tables shoved in small kitchens, or, when nothing else is available, a floor or back yard sufficed. Today we have a dedicated table in a dining room. But this has not always been the case.

Americans eat one in five meals in their cars. One in four of us eats fast food at least once a day. The average American household spends the same amount of money on fast food as it does on groceries. The average time spent eating together with family sixty years ago was ninety minutes each day. In 2016, the average family spent only twelve minutes a day eating with others.[26]

Many artistic images of hell (Bosch, Sartre, Hopper, and others) include someone eating alone at a table. T. S. Eliot wrote in his 1949 play *The Cocktail Party*, "Hell is oneself. Hell is alone, the other figures in it, merely projections. There is nothing to escape from and nothing to escape to. One is always alone."[27] Today we might even imagine someone sitting at a table alone, eating a simple meal, while scrolling through social media on a smartphone. We need the presence of others to help us avoid the hellish experience of loneliness and its debilitating effects on our lives. Intentionally gathering for regular meals with those closest to us helps combat these possibilities and lessens their impact on our well-being.

When you gather to eat with others, I challenge you to free yourself from as many distractions as possible. Our days are filled with smartphones, computers, televisions, and various other concerns. We are connected to our employers, social networks, and global news without rest. Research has shown the impact of mobile devices on our lives in recent years, and people can now see how looking at our smartphones, and thus attempting to divide our attention between multiple places, can fracture our presence in our lives and in the lives of others. When gathering around the table with the purpose of connection, we must limit distractions and focus our attention on those gathered with us.

In an effort to help focus our attention to each other at the table, my family intentionally dedicated our table as a space free from as many distractions as possible. For us this means no television in the background, and all smart devices are left in other rooms. At most, we might have music playing in the background. This creates a time entirely focused on each other. The table becomes a place where we talk and share our lives with one another. These conversations are not always deep or life-changing. My wife and I share a table with a nine-year-old boy and a twelve-year-old girl, after all. Our conversations in recent months have included Lego, school bullies, video games, mythical creatures, television show plots, internet safety, music lyrics, and a debate about whether Percy Jackson or Harry Potter is cooler. Sometimes we go entire meals without anyone saying much of anything. Some meals are spent begging our children to sit up and eat one more vegetable. We also have meals where we laugh to the point our cheeks hurt or shed tears that run so freely they drip onto the table. The table receives them all—every conversation, emotion, spilled drink, and prayer of welcome to Christ amidst the chaos. But none of these would be possible if we sat watching television or checking our notifications.

Experiment with extending your table to the world around you a little at a time. Invite a neighbor over for dinner. Encourage a co-worker to stop by for an evening dessert. Ask that family you see only at little league games, scouts, and school functions to have a lunch play date. Perhaps on the bolder side, invite the homeless guy you drive past every day on your way to work over for dinner. When you start to extend your table to others, do so with grace and courage. The table provides space for grace. When you host such dining opportunities, you extend the Christian principle of hospitality and mercy. You extend Christ's presence into the lives of others. All we can do is open our tables to others and see what happens.

In *Faithful Presence*, David Fitch reflects on Mark 6:30-44. Here, Jesus sees a crowd of thousands in need of direction. The disciples see a crowd that needs to quickly disperse so they can go into the nearby towns for dinner. Jesus, in no uncertain terms, directs the disciples to host the crowd by saying, "You give them something to eat" (Mark 6:37). Jesus wants the disciples to host the table. The disciples immediately begin to think they need to do all the work, take control of the situation, and provide from their own meager resources. Jesus takes over to show them what he really wants: "He asks how much food they have and tells them to bring the food they have. Nothing more, nothing less. So they bring to Jesus what they find among the crowd: five loaves and two fish. They in essence bring what they have as an abundance of the kingdom in Jesus. He *takes* the loaves of fish, *blesses* and *breaks* them, and *gives* it to the disciples for distribution." And everyone was filled with an abundance left over.[28]

When we open our homes and serve as hosts, we do not need to think we need to do all the work. We cannot initiate the kingdom of God, because it is not ours to initiate. It belongs to God. "Christians do not need to seek control in order to make things come out right. Instead, we are invited to identify the kingdom of God in the midst of our cracked earthen encounters."[29] We are called to see the table as a liminal space where the kingdom of God and earth meet. At the table, we take time to behold others as image bearers of God. We cannot control the outcomes of each table experience, but we can dwell in the experience with others.[30] Doing so means becoming active participants with Jesus as he takes, breaks, blesses, and gives to those at the table in order to reveal his kingdom on earth as it is in heaven. We must then bring what we have and allow Jesus to do the rest.

Conclusion

Feasts—from the garden to the heavenly banquet and into Revelation, where the new heaven and the new earth present the tree of life—fill the Bible. We also get to participate in that story right now. As Tim Chester reminds us, "The Son of Man came eating and drinking. It's not complicated. True, it's not always easy—it involves invading your space or going to places where you don't feel comfortable. But it's not complicated."[31] Eating with others is not complicated. In opening you up to other people in whole new ways and calling you to grow and examine your walk with Jesus, it can get messy. Understanding the impact of meals forces us to examine how power dynamics, geopolitical conflicts, and our myopic pursuit of homogeneity withhold food and hospitality from others.

Community makes us whole. Adam's incompletion without a partner appears as the only thing God labeled as "not good" in the creation narratives in Genesis 1–2. Gathering around the table a community subverts the norm of our culture and rebels against the standard. In a culture that values rapid change, echo chamber silos, quick lives, and fast food, slowing down long enough to eat a meal at a table with others is countercultural. In a country where ethnic, political, and economic divisions strongly exist, taking a moment to share a table with fellow congregants and neighbors creates peace in an otherwise chaotic environment.

Eating meals with others is not always convenient or easy. Setting the dining room table every night for a home-cooked meal is not always practical. But finding ways to gather is important. Besides, the food tastes so good, why would you say no?

NOTES

1. C. Christopher Smith and John Pattison, *Slow Church: Cultivating Community in the Patient Way of Jesus* (Downers Grove, IL: InterVarsity Press, 2014), 200–201.
2. David E. Fitch, *Faithful Presence: Seven Disciplines That Shape the Church for Mission* (Downers Grove, IL: InterVarsity Press, 2016), 24.
3. Fitch, *Faithful Presence*, 25.
4. Paul Trebilco, *Self-Designations and Group Identity in the New Testament* (Cambridge: Cambridge University Press, 2012), 21–22.

5. Alan Kreider, *The Patient Ferment of the Early Church: The Improbable Rise of Christianity in the Roman Empire* (Grand Rapids, MI: Baker Academic, 2016), 2.

6. Scot McKnight, *A Fellowship of Differents: Showing the World God's Design for Life Together* (Grand Rapids, MI: Zondervan, 2015), 91.

7. Jon Tyson and Heather Grizzle, *A Creative Minority: Influencing Culture through Redemptive Participation* (self-published, 2016), 17.

8. Kreider, *Patient Ferment of the Early Church*, 39–40.

9. James K. A. Smith, *Imagining the Kingdom: How Worship Works, Cultural Liturgies*, Vol. 2 (Grand Rapids, MI: Baker Academic, 2013), 98.

10. Tim Chester, *A Meal with Jesus: Discovering Grace, Community, & Mission around the Table* (Wheaton, IL: Crossway, 2011), 12.

11. Ibid.

12. Robert J. Karris, *Eating Your Way Through Luke's Gospel* (Collegeville, MN: Liturgical Press, 2006), 97.

13. Dennis E. Smith, *From Symposium to Eucharist: The Banquet in the Early Christian World* (Minneapolis, MN: Fortress Press, 2009), 2.

14. "Dinner with Jesus and Paul," The BAS Library, August 24, 2015, https://members.bib-arch.org/bible-review/20/4/7.

15. Smith, *From Symposium to Eucharist*, 9.

16. Craig Blomberg, *Contagious Holiness: Jesus' Meals with Sinners, New Studies in Biblical Theology 19* (Downers Grove, IL: InterVarsity, 2005), 90.

17. Andrew B. McGowan, *Ancient Christian Worship: Early Church Practices in Social, Historical, and Theological Perspective* (Grand Rapids, MI: Baker Academic, 2014), 20–22.

18. Paul F. Bradshaw and Maxwell E. Johnson, *The Eucharistic Liturgies: Their Evolution and Interpretation* (Collegeville, MN: Liturgical Press, 2012), 3.

19. Bradshaw and Johnson, 2.

20. Smith, *From Symposium to Eucharist*, 133–35.

21. John J. Collins and Daniel C. Harlow, eds., *The Eerdmans Dictionary of Early Judaism* (Grand Rapids, MI: Eerdmans, 2010), 924–26.

22. Blomberg, *Contagious Holiness*, 93. For a fuller study on the idea of contagious impurity and contagious holiness, see 65–163.

23. Bradshaw and Johnson, *The Eucharistic Liturgies*, 9.

24. Mark introduces a unique writing style here that my seminary professor called a "Markan sandwich." Mark will begin this section by introducing one story, walk away from it and tell a completely new story from beginning to end, and then conclude the first story. This passage has Jesus' family appear concerned for his well-being, a new scene emerges with Jesus at a dinner table debating, then his family reemerges to tie everything together.

25. McGowan, *Ancient Christian Worship*, 19–64.

26. Leonard I. Sweet, *From Tablet to Table: Where Community Is Found and Identity Is Formed* (Colorado Springs, CO: NavPress, 2014), 9–10.

27. See https://en.wikiquote.org/wiki/The_Cocktail_Party.

28. Fitch, *Faithful Presence*, 57.

29. Dan White, *Love Over Fear: Facing Monsters, Befriending Enemies, and Healing Our Polarized World* (Chicago: Moody Publishers, 2019), 174.

30. White, 174–78.

31. Chester, *A Meal with Jesus*, 15–16.

3

Shaped by the Narrative

I enjoy a good story. I especially enjoy a book or television series. I like a narrative with many parts that connect into a whole. My favorites capture the imagination and transport the reader or viewer into a whole other reality, a place where time and space and people are different from our existence. To immerse myself for several hours or even a few minutes at a time in another realm of possibility creates a sense of joy and abandon I don't find in other forms of entertainment or relaxation.

My favorite series contain multiple volumes with a clear beginning and end with a grand adventure in between. I like to buy the complete sets of books; their spines tell the whole story in key words and titles on my shelf. Books and movies like the Harry Potter series, the Lord of the Rings trilogy, and the Star Wars saga become places of wonder and possibility. I find myself identifying with characters. I want to be a wise, perceptive, brave, and intelligent person to whom others come to for counsel and comfort, like Dumbledore, Gandolf, or Yoda. However, I find myself most like Ron Weasley, Sam Wise, or Chewbacca, a goofy-looking loyal friend who supports the main characters but is not the hero. I like the mystique, heritage, and adventure of the Hogwarts castle, Middle Earth, or a massive spaceship. I have often imagined our places of higher education, institutional bodies, and local congregations being much like a well-hidden castle or planet. These are unique and special places where hopes, traditions, gifts, and education are shared freely, allowing students to move from that place fully prepared to live in a world of wonder. I find myself wondering what it would look like to be so in tune with the living Spirit of God around us in a similar way these characters tune in to the mystical forces in their various fictional narratives.

Chicago-area Anglican pastor and author Aaron Damiani loves a good story as well. During his youth, his family would gather each week for movie night. Zorro was his favorite story. "I was so enthralled by Zorro that I wanted to jump inside the TV and become part of the story. But even more so, I wanted the story I was watching to jump outside the TV and transform my life. I wanted to become the type of person who could confront evil men and wield a sword like Zorro."[1] This is the power of a good story. Good stories draw us deep into the narrative until we find ourselves participating in the story. A good narrative transforms to the point of turning us into new people. The right narratives can shape us into accurate image-bearing people of God. The wrong narratives can lead us down paths of distortion and corruption that turn us into beasts.

Stories ground our identity as human. We always need and search for a good narrative. Stories help us think through the biggest questions in our world, especially those related to identity. Questions like, "What's going on here?" "What am I to do?" and "Who am I?" are best explained in narrative. Humans are natural storytellers not because we love a good tale or because we have an insatiable need for entertainment, but rather because we think narratively. We can answer questions like "What am I to do?" only if we can answer the more important question, "Of what story or stories do I find myself a part?"[2]

When I speak of narrative, I am not referring exclusively to the fictional stories I love. Narrative is defined as "a spoken or written account of connected events; a story."[3] Yes, a narrative can refer to a fictional story, but a narrative also refers to a nonfictional telling or retelling of events. In its most basic form, narrative has a plot, characters, and a setting. Something happened to someone someplace. The storyteller or the author recounts these events, nonfiction or fictional.

Narratives, especially those we pursue, shape our lives. There are a countless number of narratives in our world. We get to choose some narratives, while others are chosen for us. Some narratives we can abandon, and others we cannot escape. Narratives can speak truth into our lives, enlightening our sense of time, place, purpose, and identity. Lies and deception shape other narratives and create in us a false understanding, impacting our view of the world and ourselves. These narratives almost always end up crushing our souls. Sometimes, we hold the power to influence our narratives and can act upon them at will. Sometimes, we do not have a say in our narratives and watch voicelessly as they unfold. All these narratives combine to shape our identity and worldviews. These narratives shape and are in turn shaped by the contexts in which they are formed. An American context creates narratives different from Asian contexts. A woman's narrative differs from a man's narrative. The narrative of a person of a racial minority will differ from that of a person of a racial majority. A person with wealth and power or one seeking such things will have a different narrative than one who does not. As participants in these narratives, we construct the unique narrative of our lives, giving meaning and purpose to our existence and the world.

With so many narratives acting upon us it is no wonder one of life's biggest question asks how to best prioritize these narratives. Most rely on context, which and makes choosing one universal answer impossible. Perhaps awareness of their presence is enough. But within our varied contexts, is there a primary narrative that will help give shape to how we engage, understand, and combine all the other narratives in our life? Is there a grand narrative in which we are invited to participate?

For thousands of years and for billions of people across multiple cultural contexts, the answer to this question takes form in the narrative of the Bible. For Christians, this includes both the Hebrew Bible (Old Testament) and the Christian New Testament. Understanding the Bible as narrative helps us better engage with the complete story. When referring to the Bible as narrative, we simply state that it tells a story about God. The Bible consists of a single cohesive story with multiple authors written across hundreds of years. The Bible has a plot that tells the story of the universe from creation to consummation. The Bible tells about a multitude of characters, the most significant being Jesus. The Bible's story is told across thousands of years and includes a variety of settings primarily focused around the Near East and the Mediterranean world.

Nonprofit film studio and podcast *The Bible Project* cofounders Tim Mackie and Jonathan Collins describe the Bible as "a unified story that leads to Jesus. This diverse collection of ancient books overflows with wisdom for our modern world. As we let the biblical story speak for itself, we believe the message of Jesus will transform individuals and entire communities."[4] New Testament scholar Scot McKnight describes the Bible as a large story held together by a series of smaller wiki-stories that are like smaller versions of the large story that serve as comments on or examples of the larger story of the Bible.[5] Old Testament scholar John Goldingay observes that the beginnings of both the Hebrew Bible and the New Testament of the Christian Bible defy expectations of any religious book. "Each begins by telling a story, doing so at some length, and doing so more than once. They take this form because the essence of the faith in both Testaments is not direct teaching about God or advice about prayer or moral instruction, but an account of what God has done, which then is the clue to formulating the teaching and the advice and the instruction."[6]

The Bible, as a narrative, contains a plot, characters, and settings and relays a series of stories by multiple authors. These authors used every literary device at their disposal to tell the story of God engaging the world. They used prose discourse, elaborate metaphors, powerful poetry, wisdom literature, historical chronologies, and prophetic images to tell a single powerful story. This book cannot outline the entirety of the deeply rich story told in Scripture. However, a summary might help us understand the overarching story within Scripture.

The New Narrative

The story begins with chaos and disorder. God speaks order into the chaos and begins to create the known universe. Like a master builder creating a house, God goes about creating all the things necessary for God's dwelling place. This creative process reveals an active and present God in the created heavens and earth. God dwells within each part of the created world. In a triumphant crescendo, God creates humanity in the image of God. Humans are designed for fellowship with God, creation, and one another, just as the Father, Son, and Holy Spirit are in constant communion with one another. Humans act as stewards and co-creators with God in this mutually shared dwelling place, ruling over and creatively cultivating the garden.

Somewhere along the way another narrative attempts to unravel the original purpose. A mysterious serpent makes its way into the garden and convinces the humans to live by a different narrative based on deception and half-truths. This false narrative tempts the humans into believing they need the responsibility of choosing good and evil. As a result of choosing this new narrative—one that attempts to usurp the authority of God—humans damaged their relationship with God, creation, and one another. They can no longer dwell with God in creation as they once did. Humans continue a downward spiral of suspicion and violence toward one another and creation until they attempt to create for themselves a place of power and self-determination in Babylon. But this only leads to frustration and dispersion across the earth.

Despite this damaged relationship, God never ceases to dwell with God's people and creation, even if the dynamics have changed. Instead God pursues a plan of redemption and restoration, one in which God is significantly and personally involved. For example, God makes a covenant promise that allows people to live into the original narrative. Abraham and his descendants have the opportunity to embody the narrative of God in a way that grants them the ability to become a people who serve as a light to the nations. This family is called to be a people who serve as examples of how a life focused on the right narrative demonstrates what right relationship with God, creation, and one another means. The rest of the Bible tells how Abraham's descendants regularly fall victim to the same deceitful narrative the first humans believed and how God refuses to let that be the final word.

The descendants of Abraham become a great nation that finds itself in bondage in the land of Egypt. God demonstrates God's presence by freeing them from slavery and leading them toward the land promised to Abraham generations earlier. God continues to guide and directly instruct the people on how to live out the first narrative and renews the covenant promise with the nation of Israel at Mount Sinai. God's laws and teachings show that people may govern themselves and live out the narrative of the people of God's kingdom. Just as all the humans before them, the people failed to pay heed to the intended narrative and instead embraced a false one.

After a period when a variety of judges repeatedly rescued Israel from local calamities, Israel asked for a human king. The desire to usurp God's leadership came even in the form of desiring human leadership over God. God relents to their cries but warns them through the prophets that human leaders always disappoint. Even the best kings who love others and are filled with divine wisdom eventually become victims of believing and creating false narratives. The people eventually build a massive temple, and God blesses the building with God's presence to demonstrate faithfulness to the narrative even when the people fail. Israel's prophets warn that if the people turn their hearts away, rather than embrace the intended narrative and be a light to the nations, they would lose their land, their nation, and their freedom, as did the first garden dwellers.

Tragically, the people did turn their hearts away from God, and the nation suffered an exile in Babylon. The prophets were right. But the prophecy did not end here. According to the prophets, hope was on the horizon and, despite the horrors of the exile and the seeming end of the narrative, the people could still redeem the original narrative. The prophets promised that God would send a new leader called a "messiah" to Israel, a Son of Man, who would rule in the context of the proper narrative and as a victim to the false narrative.

God sent Jesus, through the line of David and Abraham and Adam, to embody the proper narrative on God's behalf as Messiah. God became flesh to be the very presence of God in our midst. Jesus claimed he would bring all the promises from God to completion and that he alone lived the intended narrative on behalf of Abraham's descendants and on behalf of the rest of the world. He confronted the false narratives of power, greed, suffering, hatred, anger, insecurity, self-determination, and others. He reminded those who would listen that the original narrative was one built on love of God and love of neighbor and right relationship with creation. Acts of love, service, mercy, creative stewardship, trust, forgiveness, and many other God-centered responsibilities marked people shaped by the true narrative.

Even though Jesus exemplified the intended narrative through his actions, and though he summoned all to his table to experience relief from spiritual and physical hunger, brokenness, and shame, Abraham's descendants and Roman power brokered a deal in an attempt to remove the Son of God from the world. They feared his teachings, authority, and power as well as how he challenged their false narratives. In response, they killed Jesus by stripping him of his clothes and crucifying him on a cross. The echoes of the naked garden dwellers covering up their bodies can be seen here in an attempt to shame Jesus. But Jesus was not ashamed, and his narrative could not be stripped away or stolen by usurpers.

Jesus held all the false narratives that surround us on his cross—the ones that lie and tell us we have no value and do not deserve love; that normalize power and violence as part of the world; that using others for our own gain and personal satisfaction is acceptable; that what happens behind closed doors does not affect our souls; that excluding others from community for fear of what they may do is part of reasonable safety measures; that we alone have the power to determine what is good and what is evil; that death is the final word.

Jesus put an end to these narratives, and revealed the one true narrative, by sacrificing himself on the cross. Jesus reversed the narratives of lies and their consequences and started a new narrative. The resurrection of Jesus was the beginning of a new narrative of peace, reconciliation, and restoration.

Nobody saw it coming, not even the most intimate disciples of Jesus. For they were, as we still are, befuddled by the false narratives around us, making it difficult to believe and understand Jesus' new narrative. When God raised Jesus from the dead, God started a whole new creation narrative marked by new life and not death. To demonstrate this life, Jesus revealed his resurrected self to many people, teaching, encouraging, and eating with them. Jesus was summoned to the right hand of God as the Messiah of Abraham's descendants and the savior of the rest of the world.

The narrative will eventually conclude with the creation of a new heaven and new earth, a place where God's dwelling presence is so all-encompassing that there is no need for a temple or church. This narrative concludes with restoration to all things, where all people worship and submit to God, and people are once again in right relationship with God, creation, and one another.

This story invites us to participate in it. All of humanity has been called to see the old narratives as lies, and instead embrace the new narrative of life, peace, grace, and transformation with Jesus as king. God continues to call people together into communities that submit to this new narrative, excluding all others. These members form clusters of gathered believers called the church. God has sent the Holy Spirit to guide and transform these communities of faith into people shaped by the narrative of loving God and loving others. Followers of the new narrative, as well as these communities of faith now, share responsibility with Abraham's descendants and the first humans to live out as witnesses to the new narrative of the kingdom of God. They do this by knowing the narrative intimately, by embodying this narrative in their contexts, and by telling the narrative to others.

Reading the New Narrative in Community Formationally

Reading Scripture in the context of a community is a powerful experience. We need the story of Scripture as our foundation, since the stories we consume shape us. The early church gathered for fellowship, meals, prayer, and reexamining Scripture in addition to learning from the teachings of the apostles. For them, this meant the Hebrew Bible and the letters available to them. As gathered communities, they read Scripture and sought to understand their meaning, considering the reality of the resurrected Jesus in the context of their own local communities. They read Scripture and the letters aloud around dinner tables and discussed their implication as a community. When they read the text aloud, they heard it as a narrative with Jesus as the focal point and in which they as followers of Jesus actively participated in the forward movement of the plot.

There are a couple of different ways to read the Bible: for information and for formation. When we read the Bible for information, we search for details, facts, historical significance, literary connections, language translation, and other important information contained in Scripture. Informational reading focuses on the mastery of facts for application and interpretation generally communicated in a linear fashion. This type of reading aims to educate for the purpose of academic works such as commentaries, books, articles, teaching, or personal growth. This is an important and vital way to read Scripture. We need informational reading to gain key insights into the narrative and context of Scripture. But it is not the only, and possibly not the best, way to approach the Bible for living in the ways of Jesus.

Another way to read Scripture includes the formation approach. Approaching the Bible formationally means we intentionally read in search of a transformative encounter with God. We read the Bible as a narrative to inhabit, not just a set of historical and literary facts for analysis. Formational reading focuses on how to fully inhabit our own stories. The quality, rather than the quantity, of formational reading carries more weight. This type of biblical reading shapes the reader through contemplation of Scripture in community with others. It is not a process of mastery over the text but instead allows the Bible to gain mastery over our communities and ourselves. The Bible can reach inside to renew our hearts and transform our minds. The narrative of Scripture is not a manual filled with "six steps to a better you" programs. Rather, it summons us to dwell deep inside the narrative of Jesus redeeming creation and bringing all things into fulfillment in himself.

Scot McKnight identifies some common errors in approaching biblical text without the proper context of narrative. He believes that somewhere along the way we as Christian readers stopped reading the Bible as a story. The difficulty and time-consuming nature of narratives depreciates motivation. You must understand context, where you are in the narrative, and how previous parts shape a passage or how it in turn shapes what comes later. Instead, over the past few centuries, we started creating shortcuts that broke the narrative down into smaller, more easily handled categories. We want to focus on laws and rules, blessings and promises, and bite-sized moral codes.[7] With constant reminders of the Bible's narrative nature, we can guard against potential errors like creating shortcuts. The presence of God fills every part of a narrative and allowing this presence to shape us can then reshape our imaginations and worldviews. The Bible, when read formationally, opens space for us to see the world differently.

Additionally, we should read the Bible in a community with other followers of Jesus. We cannot hope to gain the full impact of the narrative of Scripture when we read it alone. In his classic work *Life Together,* Dietrich Bonhoeffer reminds us of the importance of reading Scripture in the context of a community of faith.

> When one person is struck by the Word, he speaks it to others. God has willed that we should seek to find His living Word in the witness of a brother, in the mouth of man. Therefore, the Christian needs another Christian who speaks God's Word to him. He needs him again and again when he becomes uncertain and discouraged, for by himself he cannot help himself without belying the truth. He needs his brother man as a bearer and proclaimer of the divine word of salvation . . . And that also clarifies the goal of all Christian community: they meet one another as bringers of the message of salvation.[8]

We need our brothers and sisters in Christ to help us be shaped properly by the narrative of Scripture. Left alone to our personal devotional readings, we will quickly fall victim to the type of errors McKnight and others warn us about in reading Scripture.

Reading Scripture aloud and discussing it with a small group of fellow followers of Jesus helps us engage with the Bible differently than when reading it silently or alone. Reading alone, silently or aloud, is important, and we should spend time daily reflecting on Scripture for the purposes of information and formation. But reading alone should be guided by our times of community reading, reflection, and prayer.

As discussed above, the surrounding narrative frameworks shape us. These narratives create lenses through which we view the world and Scripture. These lenses limit our ability to interact fully with the biblical narrative. When left to our own devices we tend to skip parts of the Bible we don't like or have difficulty understanding. We might create a theology of God that looks a lot like the person in the mirror, rather than a true representation of God. We might not see how a text impacts multiple lives and contexts when we never share our reading experiences with others. We are better at reading the Bible and better at living out the Christian experience when we do so in the context of a community.

Reading the Bible with others can help identify limitations in our perspectives as well as limitations in the perspective of others. We need the voice and interaction of other believers, and the different narratives and new perspectives they bring to the text, as we fully grow in Jesus. We must listen to each other and discern together how the Bible's narrative can be lived in each of our contexts. When we read together, we pull on the gifts of all those present. In a reading group we get both the much-needed information provided by our teachers who inform us of the historical, literary, and contextual issues in the text. Equally important, we also hear from the collective wisdom of others who help us faithfully live out the narrative in our unique situations. As we sit around the table in community, we trust that the Spirit of God will work through our collective gifts, guiding us toward living into the narrative of Scripture together as the people of God.

Dwelling in the Word

Telling and retelling the biblical narrative grounds the way Christians interpret their experiences. We need to be reminded who we are sometimes. Listening to Scripture helps us do this. We need to be reminded who God is and what God is doing in the world. Scripture helps us with this too. We need to read Scripture as a narrative with a community of believers, so we can be reminded of who God is, how God is moving in the world, and how we fit into the story.

Followers of Jesus have read Scripture numerous ways over time with context, purpose, and access to Scriptures constructing their approaches. In our current context, dwelling in the Word[9] provides a powerful and helpful way for followers of Jesus, and those curious about the Christian life, to engage the biblical narrative as a community for the purpose of formation. Dwelling in the Word offers space for those involved to engage the Word. Each person present is encouraged to listen to Scripture and reflect on God's movement in the text. I find dwelling in the Word to be the most effective way to read Scripture in a community.

Based on the tradition of *lectio divina*,[10] dwelling in the Word is a process of listening prayerfully to Scripture in the context of community, or "a way of letting God address us through Scripture, rather than using Scripture only as a tool for imparting additional information or confirming existing beliefs. Dwelling in the Word invites the Holy Spirit to enliven a biblical text among us, so that we become aware of and responsive to what God is doing. This is a practice of listening to God through the text and through one another."[11] This process encourages the reading community to make listening for God in Scripture a habit in their community: "God invites us to attend and discern, but in a humble, tentative way. . . . Our learning may be awkward at first. . . . It is why we don't try to do this listening and discerning on our own; we commit to living in a church community, in humble submission to one another."[12]

To hear God best requires a community where fellow brothers and sisters in Christ help each other discern and respond to what God might be saying to each person in the group. Recent Christian tradition has emphasized the responsibility of each individual follower of Jesus to read and interpret Scripture. Historically, the church has held individual discernment in tension with community discernment as a vital part of healthy Bible reading and application. Dwelling in the Word allows the participants to exercise both individual freedom and community responsibility.

There are differences between dwelling in the Word and Bible study. Bible studies are guided by leaders using study guides, commentaries, outlines, or other teaching aids. The purpose of Bible studies aims for a class to learn ways to understand the text from the leader, study guide, or video. Bible study exists as a vital discipline within the life of the church, and Christians should be engaged in continuing their education in the historical, literary, and contextual settings of the Bible for their own edification and the edification of the church. Without proper knowledge of the context and information about biblical narratives, formational reading can potentially stray into the allegorical.

As a formational approach, dwelling in the Word requires participants to sit patiently before Scripture in a spirit of receptivity. Dwelling does not offer a how-to guide in creating biblical commentaries but presents a way to develop habits of listening for God's words to those in the group through Scripture: "We might say Bible study is how *we read* the text; dwelling is letting the text *read us*. Dwelling involves practicing our way into a new understanding, rather than understanding our way into a new practice."[13] Dwelling in the Word requires a habit where participants engage Scripture while in a community to listen for the voice of God.

Here is how to engage in a Dwelling in the Word reading:[14]

The community gathers to read a small portion of the biblical narrative. It might be beneficial before reading the passage to quickly remind those gathered where they are in the narrative to help them understand the context of the passage. This is an example of how information helps to guide formation.

Once the group chooses a passage, the gathered community asks two people to read the text aloud. Ideally this would include two people who represent the larger community, such as a male voice and a female voice or an adult and a child. This variety helps us hear the text differently and pay attention to the message.

As the passage is read aloud the rest of the community listens for words, phrases, and ideas that stand out in the reading. Listeners can follow along with their own Bibles or printed copies of the passage. They might close their eyes and attempt to visualize the passage and focus on the spoken words. There might be an artistic representation of the passage such as a painting, sculpture, or musical score for people to look at or listen to while the passage is read. Ultimately, the group should listen to the words read aloud and think about the text formationally.

Once the first reader finishes, a moment of silence follows for people to reflect on what they heard. Listeners can write down the word or phrase that stood out, underline them in their Bibles or printed copies, write notes, draw pictures, or anything else they need to help them in the reflection process.

After a few minutes, the second person begins reading, and again the rest of the group listens as best they can for what the Spirit is saying. Once the second reading finishes, another moment of silence and reflection follows.

After a few minutes, a leader asks people to share what they felt God said to them during this Scripture reading. If the group is small, people can take turns sharing as a whole group. This is an exciting way to hear what God said to each person and affirm the working of the Spirit. If the group is larger, have participants pair off into groups of two to three people to share what spoke to them in the reading. As you listen to your fellow readers share, pay attention and focus on what they say. Affirm their reflections. After several moments of sharing, a leader can ask for everyone's attention again and have someone from each group share what their partner heard from the text. This way of sharing helps us pay attention to what others heard from God as they read and then recommunicate that with the rest of the group. The partner will then do the same for the other person.

This dwelling in the Word exercise allows people to really listen to God's action in their lives. It creates space for participants to share how God speaks to them as individuals and as a group. Dwelling in the Word is a simple practice that requires little informational expertise in the biblical narrative. It is a gentle way for participants to begin the habit of Scripture reading with others in their local community. It helps participants ask the dual questions of "What is God saying to me individually?" and "What is God saying to us as a faith community?"

Conclusion

Narratives give shape to the world, helping us see what is beautiful and just, what it means to be human, and how we should live in community. The various narratives around us compete for our attention and seek primacy in our hearts. Some of those narratives help develop meaningful self-images, morality, and purpose. Other narratives damage us and the world. If we do not have an all-encompassing grand narrative available to us, we will quickly become overwhelmed and crushed by our experiences.

The Bible is the ultimate narrative that gives shape and meaning to all the other narratives that seek to influence us as individuals and as communities. When we study the Bible through the formational approach, in addition to allowing the narrative of the Bible in its entirety to form us, we begin to see where the other narratives in our lives need adjustment. When we read the narrative of Scripture as a community by dwelling in the Word, we are able to see more clearly how the Spirit of God works in our midst. Reading the Bible as a narrative gives us the complete and full story of salvation and transforms us through the whole gospel.

NOTES

1. Aaron Damiani, *The Good of Giving Up: Discovering the Freedom of Lent* (Chicago, IL: Moody Publishers, 2017), 24.
2. James K. A. Smith, *Imagining the Kingdom: How Worship Works*, Cultural Liturgies, Vol. 2 (Grand Rapids, MI: Baker Academic, 2013), 194–96.
3. See https://www.lexico.com/en/definition/narrative.
4. "Our Mission," The Bible Project, accessed March 16, 2020, https://thebibleproject.com/about/.
5. Scot McKnight, *The Blue Parakeet: Rethinking How You Read the Bible* (Grand Rapids, MI: Zondervan, 2008), 63-79.
6. John Goldingay, *Reading Jesus's Bible: How the New Testament Helps Us Understand the Old Testament* (Grand Rapids, MI: Eerdmans, 2017), 5.
7. McKnight, *Blue Parakeet*, 42–54.
8. Dietrich Bonhoeffer, *Life Together* (New York: HarperCollins, 2005), 22–23.
9. I first learned of "Dwelling in the Word" from Dr. Alan Roxburgh in a conference in Denver, Colorado, in 2009.
10. Lectio divina (literally "divine reading") is a process of slowly reading and prayerfully reflecting on short passages of Scriptures multiple times. It is a practice dating back to sixth-century Benedictine monasteries.
11. Alan J. Roxburgh, *Joining God, Remaking Church, Changing the World: The New Shape of the Church in Our Time* (New York: Morehouse, 2015), 60.
12. Roxburgh, *Joining God, Remaking Church, Changing the World*, 61.
13. Roxburgh, *Joining God, Remaking Church, Changing the World*, 62.
14. See Appendix A for a step-by-step process.

4

Listening

I live in a modest starter home neighborhood near a state-protected forest and creek. My neighbors and I get to enjoy the feeling of living in a semi-secluded wooded space adjacent to farmland with all the benefits of living near an urban center. It's a quiet space where kids can run and ride bikes and play safely. It is not uncommon to see several neighbors chatting on sidewalks or driveways. But we are still just a small Midwest neighborhood near the heart of the largest city in our region. When guests come to visit, they are often surprised by the impressive, picturesque garden worthy of a *Better Homes and Gardens* magazine cover that's between my home and my next-door neighbors.

My neighbors are avid gardeners. Their garden is home to the best vegetables and fruits in the county. Over the years they have grown various forms of corn, tomatoes, peppers, berries, gourds, asparagus, peas, lettuce, carrots, and more. They have planted fruit trees, deciduous trees, and evergreens. They have annual and perennial flowers in beds, retaining walls, and containers. Each year they rotate their crops to keep the soil fresh and healthy and even have their own compost pile to supplement tired soil. They love to spend their after-work hours and weekends toiling in the garden to prepare, maintain, and harvest their produce. The best part is that they lovingly share their produce with the neighborhood. I have not had to buy tomatoes, green beans, and most importantly, grape jelly, in years.

One of the defining features of my neighbors' garden is the grapevine that runs along our fence line. It is at least thirty feet long and home to the finest jelly-making grapes in the Midwest. It is also a gathering place. It attracts people as effectively as it attracts the Japanese beetles who seek to devour the leaves. Everyone in our neighborhood has congregated around this grapevine at one time or another. My neighbors, family, and friends have spent countless hours talking and sharing stories near the grapevine. We talk about safe neighborly things like the weather, school schedules, neighborhood changes, and whose turn it is to cut the grass in the common space. We also sometimes have difficult conversations about family challenges, work-related pressures, aging parents, death, money, politics, and Jesus and the church. Some of my most important conversations in recent years have taken place within line of sight of that grapevine.

I Heard It by the Grapevine

My experiences standing in the shadow of the grapevine have taught me the value of listening. I am not a naturally good listener. When we first moved to the neighborhood and started gathering around the grapevine, I realized I mixed people up. I would get names wrong or attach stories to the wrong person. It was a problem. I spent time thinking of something interesting to talk about and didn't listen to what others said. I tended to want to speak more than listen. I wanted to help solve problems instead of sitting with people in pain. I want to make dad jokes and preacher puns rather than engage in difficult conversations.

What I realized most is that I did not love people the way I should. I did not listen in a way that demonstrated I cared about them. As an ordained minister who has spent many hours in continuing education events and a consumer of multivolume books on listening and pastoral presence, I have disciplined myself to at least look like I am paying attention when others speak. It turns out no matter how many articles or seminars on active listening you consume, if your goal is to demonstrate how good you are at active listening, your attention is focused on the process and not actually listening to the person.

Once I realized what was happening, I committed to being more present with my neighbors when we spoke. Now when people congregate near the grapevine, I ask God to help me pay attention. I ask God to help me be present as the Holy Spirit is present. I seek to truly listen and be fully present with them. I have learned more about my neighbors and others by listening than I ever did by talking. I find that if I am patient and give my attention to what my neighbors share, my depth of love and appreciation for my neighbors grows. I also recognize those days when I talk more than listen that my neighbors hear me and that encourages and validates me in turn. Listening does not mean you never speak; it means you listen first and speak out of a place of full presence. I find what I share to be more meaningful if I take the time to properly listen first.

When done well, listening can transform and ultimately grounds table life. I advocate that we learn how to become better listeners in three areas. We gather together for meals so we can more effectively listen to our contexts which includes our church and neighborhood communities. We read

Scripture as a community to improve our ability to listen to the Father, Son, and Holy Spirit. We practice storytelling to experience the life-affirming gift of being heard.

To become better listeners, we need to take a moment and reflect on what it means to truly listen. Let's look at an ancient community prayer called "listen."

Shema (Listen)

In the Gospels of Matthew and Mark, a legal expert asked Jesus which of the 613 commands found in the Torah is the most significant. Jesus responds by paraphrasing Deuteronomy 6:4 and Leviticus 19:34:

> "The most important one," answered Jesus, "is this: 'Hear, O Israel: The Lord our God, the Lord is one. Love the Lord your God with all your heart and with all your soul and with all your mind and with all your strength.' The second is this: 'Love your neighbor as yourself.' There is no commandment greater than these." (Mark 12:29-31)

With these words, Jesus summarizes from the narrative of Scripture an example of a life shaped by God. We are to love God and love others. We pursue healthy relationships with God and with other people. We cannot have one without the other.

Deuteronomy 6:4-9 is referred to as the *shema*, the Hebrew word for "listen." Jewish people have prayed this twice a day, every day, for roughly the past thirty-five hundred years. For all those reaching for their calculators, people have intentionally said this community prayer more than two-and-a-half million times. This prayer affirms the identity of God as unique and holy. It summons the community to wholly and fully love God. It challenges people to think constantly about their connection with God and others by reflecting on these words day and night, at home and away. It calls on each generation to pass these habits and beliefs onto the next generation.

The *shema* is straightforward enough: Deuteronomy 6:4 in Hebrew begins with *shema*. The entire call to love God with your heart, soul, and strength is built on the foundation of listening. This is not a big surprise. If you were to do an informational study of the word "listen" in the Bible you would discover that it appears in various forms more than fifteen hundred times. It is one of the most common words in all of Scripture. But if you look at the context in which the prayer appears, you will also discover that it is often used to describe how often people do not listen well. I guess I could be grateful that so much of Scripture mentions how poorly people listen to God and to each other. It puts me in plentiful company. A formational reading of these texts would help us recognize our need to focus more on the craft of listening.

Shema, in its most basic meaning, focuses on physical hearing. Sound waves travel through the air and bounce off various objects before finally reaching your ear. Once those waves hit your inner ear, your drum vibrates and stimulates little hairs on your cochlea that turn sound waves into electrical signals that are transmitted to your brain. Your brain then discerns them into meaningful sounds. This is an amazing process God built into our bodies. We should not take lightly the ability to hear. As Proverbs 20:12 reminds us: "Ears that *shema* and eyes that see—the LORD has made them both."

Shema, in a biblical sense, carries deeper meanings. *Shema* also means to pay attention or focus. It is about turning your attention to something new—like when a loud noise happens unexpectedly, and we instinctively face the direction of the sound to discern its cause. *Shema* also means to intentionally turn away from one focus to set our energy and efforts into another task.

With that focus, the implication of *shema* listening is to respond. We hear a sound, we turn our faces toward it, then we respond to that sound with some sort of action. For example, when we hear a sudden sound and register it as the cry of our child, we run toward the child to help. This is what it means to truly *shema*. We hear a sound, we turn our faces toward it, and then we take action by responding appropriately.

The ancient Hebrew language did not have a word for "obey" or "obedience." They used the word *shema*. Listening and doing were linked in the ancient Hebrew mind. This was true of our English words "obey" and "listen" from their origins. The words "listen" and "obey" have the same Latin root, and one could not exist without the other. The word we translate in English as "obedience" literally means "listening from below." "Obedience is a deep listening, a listening of the whole person, a hearing with your ears and with your heart and with your arms and legs."[1]

True listening requires all our attention and a response of obedience. Sometimes I tell my children to "listen up" or "listen to me." My goal for them to "listen" extends beyond sound waves and electrical signals. I hope for them to respond positively to what I say. If I say, "Listen up, it's time to get ready for bed," I hope that they then stop what they are doing, look at me, register the reality of bedtime, and proceed with the bedtime routines. If they don't start the routine I might ask, "Didn't you hear me?" Again, the point being that if they had truly heard, they would have responded in obedience. They would have (and I'm making up words now) fully *shema'd*. Exodus 19:5 puts it like this: "If you *shema* me fully and keep my covenant, then out of all the nations you will be my treasured possession." This implies that if the people of Israel really hear, listen, pay attention to, and respond to God's presence and teachings appropriately, they are keeping the covenant and (more made-up words) *shema'ing*.

Deuteronomy 6 and the fifteen hundred other appearnaces of listening in the Bible drive home the point that listening is more than an auditory experience. To *shema* faithfully requires responding to what we hear with obedience. If we do not respond, we do not *shema*. When we listen to the narrative of Scripture and allow it to shape us in a way that causes us to respond by loving God and loving others, we *shema*. When listening to other human beings we take the first steps in loving them and validating them as image bearers of God. When we listen to our communities, churches, and neighborhoods we follow the example of Jesus, who "became flesh and moved into the neighborhood" (John 1:14, MSG).

How do we know we have adequately listened? If we listen to Jesus, our response will be to love God with our hearts, souls, and strength and to love our neighbors as ourselves.

Listen to God

The prophet Elijah bursts into the biblical narrative unannounced, and with little background, in 1 Kings 17. We are told he comes from an area in Gilead called Tishbe, which means "heavily wooded area." Elijah might be the only person in the Bible who literally came out of the woodwork. We also only know the meaning of his name: "Yahweh is his God." Elijah arrives confronting Israel's current king, Ahab, whose reign is fraught with problems like idolatry, oppression, poor administration, and military failures. But for Elijah, Jezebel's—Ahab's wife's—strong support of the Canaanite deities Baal and Asherah raise the most issue.

After a three-year drought, Elijah convinces the prophet Obadiah to secure him an audience with the king. Ahab greets him with one of the greatest epithets in Scripture: "Is that you, you troubler of Israel?" (1 Kings 18:17). In response, Elijah accuses Ahab of trading loyalty to God for loyalty to Baal. He then challenges Ahab to summon all of Israel and the prophets of Baal and Asherah to a divine showdown on Mount Carmel. In the days before social media, twenty-four-hour news cycle, and billboards, heralds announced these showdowns in every town. Several weeks later, the people gather at Mount Carmel.

Once "all of Israel" and the prophets of Baal and Asherah arrive, Elijah lays down the parameters of the challenge. Elijah and the Baal worshipers will each build an altar, lay a sacrifice on top, and ask their deity to respond by consuming the sacrifice. The challenge is accepted, and they go to work. As a sporting prophet, Elijah encourages the priests of Baal to go first. They sing, dance, cut themselves, and work themselves up into a frenzy asking Baal to come and make his presence known. Elijah engages in some intense gamesmanship, taunting the prophets by suggesting that Baal is busy, away from the office on a journey, or asleep. After a round of intensified efforts, Elijah puts a stop to it and takes his turn.

Elijah calls on those around him to help set up his altar. They stack uncut rocks, gather the wood, and lay his bull upon the altar. Then Elijah calls on them to pour water over the sacrifice—in a three-year drought and arid climate, water is a precious commodity needed for survival. Yet, Elijah's unnamed helpers pour so much water on the altar it creates a pool underneath. Then, Elijah prays a simple prayer: "LORD, the God of Abraham, Isaac and Israel, let it be known today that you are God in Israel and that I am your servant and have done all these things at your command. Answer me, LORD, answer me, so these people will know that you, LORD, are God, and that you are turning their hearts back again" (1 Kings 18:36-37).

In our pursuit to be good listeners sometimes we need reminders that God also listens to us. The creator of the universe is a listener. Over and over again, we witness God hearing the prayers of God's people and responding. God hears the plight of Hagar and Hannah, Jacob and Joshua, David and Daniel, Jonah and Job, and the psalmists and the prophets. God hears the cries of God's people in slavery and moves heaven and earth to respond to their need for rescue. The most important redemption story in the Old Testament began when God heard the cries of God's people (Exodus 3:9), and it moved God into action. God *shema'd* the people, and it moved God into compassionate engagement. This is one of the most amazing and humbling realities of the cosmos. The God who spoke all things into being and has the most right to be heard and obeyed demonstrates how to listen by hearing and responding to the cries and calls of those who seek God's presence.

God *shema'd* Elijah's prayer and responded by sending down a holy fire so powerful it consumed the sacrifice, the water, and even the rocks! This authoritative display of power and presence motivated the people of Israel to *shema* in turn by repenting and worshiping God.

Elijah and his newly penitent Israelite supporters then do the unthinkable, and I have no way of reconciling their actions. I wish they had not revenge killed all those Baal and Asherah prophets. It is a lot like repenting of gluttony and then killing the chefs who made your calorie-laden dinners. Perhaps their actions brought grief to God. The story does not say God told them to take such action or how God felt about it. We are told only how Jezebel felt. In her anger, she threatens to kill Elijah for eliminating her prophets (1 Kings 19:1-2). The threat of escalating homicide sends Elijah into the wilderness in fear. He finds himself alone and suicidal under a broom tree in the middle of the desert. Then, suddenly, an angel provides him with food and drink and tells him to travel to Mount Horeb, the same mountain where God met with Moses in the form of a burning bush and where God met Israel after the exodus to establish a covenant through the giving of the law.

When Elijah climbs up the side of Mount Horeb several weeks later, he finds a nice little cave and settles in to wait. The drought ends, the crops are ready to grow again, Israel's hearts have turned back to God, and he has survived the past month on a single loaf of bread. Perhaps, in this place of reflection, Elijah repented for his violent actions at Mount Carmel. Whatever his thoughts, forty days in the wilderness increased his sensitivity enough to hear the presence of God in a new way.

As Elijah prepared to lie down for the night, the voice of God called to him in what I like to imagine was a bit of an accusatory tone: "What are you doing here, Elijah?" (1 Kings 19:9). Elijah should not be hiding in the wilderness or finding solitude in a cave. As a prophet, he should proclaim the message God gave him, but instead he ran away. Sure, Jezebel wants him dead. Perhaps she would not want this if he restrained himself from violence. Either way Elijah is on the run, but he should not be on Mount Horeb. He should be in Israel.

Elijah responds as those who isolate themselves from others often do: "I have been very zealous for the LORD God Almighty. The Israelites have rejected your covenant, torn down your altars, and put your prophets to the death. I am the only one left, and now they are trying to kill me too" (1 Kings 19:10). He believes himself to be a holy remnant swimming in a sea of heretical traitorous mercenaries.

God does not have time for Elijah's nonsense. Israel did not fully turn their back on God. Thousands of people did not begin to worship Baal, but rather remained just as faithful to Yahweh as Elijah (1 Kings 19:18). Elijah is not the only prophet left; Obadiah, who serves in the court of Ahab, has at least one hundred other prophets safely hidden in caves around Israel (1 Kings 18:4). The situation may not be good, but fear amplifies Elijah's negative feelings about it further. Elijah became overwhelmed with fear, and as a result he could not see the whole picture.

God tells Elijah to stand on the exposed face of the mountain. I'm no mountaineer, but it's easy to see the danger of standing on the face of a mountain. Weather can change in an instant, large animals roam the cliffs, footing is easily lost, high altitudes can make breathing and rational thinking difficult. Elijah forgoes the safety of his cave and his delusions to walk onto the mountain face and meet with the Maker of mountains.

When Elijah finally comes out of his cave and makes it onto the face of Mount Horeb, God appears with power. On this very mountain in Exodus 19:16-19, God settles and makes God known through winds, earthquakes, and fire to give the Law to the people—a story Elijah would certainly know by heart. But this time God spoke in a new way, and it was Elijah's task to *shema* in every sense of the word.

First, a huge wind shattered the rocks, an element familiar to God's presence. The Hebrew word *ruah* means "breath" or "wind" or "words." It was God's *ruah* that spoke creation into order and gave life to humans (Genesis 1–2). It was a mighty *ruah* that separated the Sea of Reeds for the people to walk on dry ground (Exodus 13). A mighty wind also came on the day of Pentecost as a manner of communication in different languages for the earliest Jesus followers (Acts 2). But God was not in the wind this time.

Next came an earthquake. In the psalms and the prophets, God's mighty presence often shakes the earth. For example, God shakes the earth and splits it wide open to consume

Dathan and his family when they challenged Moses (Numbers 16). When Jesus is resurrected (Matthew 28), an earthquake occurs. But God was not in the earthquake this time.

Next fire broke out on the mountain. Heat and smoke surrounded Elijah. God appears as a pillar of fire to guide the people of Israel in the wilderness. God speaks to Moses out of a burning bush on the same mountain (Exodus 3). Elijah himself witnesses God consume his altar with a holy fire just weeks earlier. The very presence of God is referred to as a consuming fire in Hebrews 12:29. But God was not in this fire either.

Then, out of the cacophony of howling winds, shifting earth, and raging flames something new happened.

Silence.

Not just quiet or calm.

An absolute, all-consuming silence teeming with the presence of God.

Elijah *heard* the silence, and he knew it was God. Elijah *shema'd* by covering his face and walking deeper into the silence.

Listening for God can lead us into some unexpected places. God can speak clearly and loudly in some obvious ways. Other times God fills the silences with God's presence. We just have a hard time hearing it. Often the winds, earthquakes, and fires raging in our souls make it difficult to listen. We sit in our caves and allow these untamed elements to rule over us and create fear and anxiety in places where there should be peace and love. If we seek their counsel, they will always push us into the wilderness where we find ourselves under broom trees wishing for death. The good news is that God will meet you under your tree and offer you new life.

Nobody would have faulted Elijah for expecting God's voice in the wind, earthquake, or fire. God has spoken through these elements in the past and would speak again in the future. It was familiar and expected. But Elijah was sensitive and discerning enough to realize God did not speak in that way this time. God comes to him so clearly that Elijah covers his face in humble submission. Have we missed the presence of God in our midst by only looking for fires, winds, and moving ground?

Discerning the presence of God is no simple task. We often miss God's presence by focusing our attention on present turbulence. But when we hear it over and above the chaos, we realize God will usher in order and peace. The ability to hear the presence of God does not immediately change our circumstances. Elijah is still a man on the run, currently sitting on a mountain under a divine weather attack. Yet the presence of God changes everything.

Elijah would finish his mountaintop experience by receiving a new calling and a word of encouragement. God reminds Elijah that he is not alone; God commissioned him to oversee a regime change, and he would not do it alone. He would find help and companionship in anointing a new prophet. He heard all of that in the sounds of silence. This prepared Elijah to face his circumstances and move forward with the presence of God.

God roars in the wind and sometimes sends an angel to deliver his message. God's presence can be felt on silent retreat, at a campground, on a subway, or in a car. God's presence acts and moves in our meaningful protests against injustices and in the quiet spaces of our prayer closets convicting us of our injustices. God listens and God speaks. If our souls pay attention, we too will experience the presence of God in our lives. If we respond to what we hear, then we have *shema'd* and will experience *shalom*.

Listen to Others

Table life pivots on the dual practices of dwelling in the Word and storytelling. Each informs the other and both hold each other through the practice of listening. Those who wish to grow in Christ must learn to listen to God and to God's people in every context. This allows us to heighten our awareness of God's actions in our local communities and world. Dietrich Bonhoeffer in *Life Together* says: "The first service that one owes to others in the fellowship consists of listening to them. Just as love of God begins with listening to His Word, so the beginning of love for the brethren is listening to them. It is God's love for us that He not only gives us His Word but also lends us His ear. So it is His work that we do for our brother when we learn to listen to him."[2]

By listening to Scripture in a community, we better understand how God acts in the biblical narrative. We also listen within our experiences as Elijah did. When listening to the stories of others, we better understand our personal and corporate participation in the kingdom of God on earth as it is in heaven. By taking turns speaking and listening, hosting and attending, reading and hearing, leading and following, we learn to be a faithful Christian community shaped by the heart of Christ. True listening allows us to share power and follow one another as we all seek to follow God together.

When we listen to others we value them just as God values them. If we believe that God loves us and eagerly seeks an interactive relationship with us, then we must believe this is true for others as well. If we believe we are to love God and love others, then we listen to others as God would listen to them and in the way we hope God hears us.

Listening to other people chips away at the space that exists between people. We can easily turn others into opponents. We elevate the good and noble in ourselves while emphasizing the suspect and scandalous in the lives of others. This creates distance—an "us" verses "them" approach to life that only divides. If we do this enough, we stop seeing other people as image bearers of God. "Jesus followers must transcend these social ghettos of self-righteousness. If we believe that all of us, even our enemies, are created in the image of God, then we must behold it."[3] The only way to truly behold another is to stop, be present, and listen to them.

Find Someone Who Really Listens to You

For the past several years, I have met with a spiritual director. A spiritual director is like a personal pastor, but more focused on spiritual development. Think formation over information. Spiritual directors offer a safe space to slow down, breathe, reflect on your story, and receive the needed support throughout one's faith journey.

My director guides me in prayer exercises, suggests books to read, and pushes me toward deeper understanding of my identity in Christ. His biggest gift to me is that he listens. When we meet, he will often begin with "What would you like to talk about today?" or "What is God doing in your life?" or my personal favorite, "How is your soul?" I do not always know what to talk about or how to frame what is going on in my spiritual life, but these questions help me to start. Next thing I know, twenty or thirty minutes have passed with me talking about the ins and outs of my relationships, ministry, and personal spiritual journey.

My spiritual director just sits there sagely, listening and encouragingly nodding his head and laughing at my lame jokes. Sometimes he will chime in with an observation such as, "This is what I hear in that story . . ." or "I can see the Spirit moving in this way . . ." When I ask him for advice, he always helps me figure out my next steps instead of giving me a list of tasks. Of course at times I wish he would give me a to-do list of activities, prayers, or Scriptures to read. But he never does because he knows I need to learn that "doing" is not the same as "being." He always listens, guides, and then listens some more, affirming or challenging my conclusions in addition to following up in our next session.

Not everyone has a spiritual director, and if you do not, I strongly suggest you investigate the opportunity. It has been one of the most important relationships in my life. I believe that most people do not have another person in their lives who truly listens to them as they deserve. We need more people in our lives who are better listeners. I encourage you to find someone who will listen to you. I also challenge you to become a better listener.

Being a good listener is not difficult. When entering a conversation, remember to make it about the other person, not you. Having a listening heart fights against the selfishness that runs so deeply in our bones. The ability to listen to others requires us releasing the desire for control that makes us want to use a conversation for our benefit rather than simply sitting with another.[4] This is not limited to difficult and heavy conversations. Good listening includes being "attentive to, immersed in, and appreciative of the everyday texture of people's lives—the buying and selling, the visiting and meeting, the going and coming."[5]

Many books and seminars out there can help sharpen your listening skills. Feel free to check them out and grow your arsenal. But remember, perhaps over anything else, that listening to others includes hearing the good and the bad, the interesting and the mundane, and all the other aspects of a person's life experience. All this guides us to recognize the divine spark in each person God has made.

Listen to Our Communities

A variety of narratives and contexts shape each of our lives. Whether we live in a small town without stoplights or in a large urban center with millions of people, God is present. As followers of Christ, we want to find ways to recognize how God dwells in our neighborhood to join God there.[6] I have had the opportunity to minister alongside multiple congregations. On any given week as a regional minister, I will help one congregation identify its next pastor, another congregation navigate a conflict, another congregation start a new ministry, and guest speak at another one. It is a wonderful ministry that allows me to engage followers of Jesus in different contexts each week. In my experience, it is easier to encourage congregations to read Scripture together and listen to one another than it is to convince them of the importance of listening for God's presence in their neighborhood communities.

I think there are a few reasons for this. First, openly admitted or not, many people mistakenly believe God is most present within the confines of a church building. For many well-meaning Christians, if a ministry does not take place in the space of a well-cared-for and beloved church building, or at least originating in such a space, then it is not really ministry. Therefore, many churches have their own versions of good community ministries that exist outside the church. Food pantries, clothing banks, community gardens, community centers, homeless shelters, sports leagues, counseling services, medical clinics, and many other services all contribute excellent opportunities for Christians to get involved in ministry. Why do we feel the need to re-create them in our church fellowship halls, basements, and gymnasiums? Is it because we have neglected to listen to our communities and thus do not know what they have to offer? Or does some sort of spiritual pride lead us to believe those places are unworthy of our partnership?

Second, we have become a commuting society. In the United States, especially, many of us commute in our cars. I remember when I first began ministry I was taught that a church will grow if it increases its parking. This means that, with more available parking, people from further away would join our church. This may or may not have worked, and it certainly created a whole new "parking team" ministry opportunity. But the truth is we commute. We might live in one corner of town and in a neighborhood or school district we like, but work in a separate part of town. We might shop at another end of town, because the grocer seems cleaner or has that special toothpaste we like. Then, we might attend church in yet another quadrant of a city, liking their praise team best. This impacts every aspect of our lives, but for the sake of local church ministry I think it is detrimental. How can a church with members from across a twenty-mile radius even begin to discern what God is doing in all the neighborhoods represented? How can members focus on God's presence in their neighborhood if they spend all their time across town shopping in another neighborhood? How can we know how to influence our communities with industry and good business practices if we seek employment in another county?

Another reason congregations hesitate at listening to their neighbors steers toward the representation of their neighborhoods in the congregation. This primarily addresses long-established congregations. Why was your church planted in the location it is in now? It is probable that a missionary, denominational body, or another local church thought that neighborhood needed another Christian congregation, so they planted a church to meet the needs of a community. Over time the community slightly shifted. New people moved in, and some of the church members may have stayed while others may have moved to another neighborhood. The church countered by creating attractional destination ministries. Youth groups, women's and men's groups, preschools, Wednesday night events, concerts, movie nights, and other ministries sought to attract people from a wide range of places outside of the local neighborhood to support the local church, its staff, and its building. Then one day the church looked up and discovered membership had dwindled and that it had not represented their neighborhood with a single member in the church.

Listening to our neighborhoods assists us participating in God's presence all around us. In *Slow Church*, C. Christopher Smith and John Pattison argue for a church that is a "distinctively local expression of the global body of Christ . . . With a commitment to place, and with gratitude for the immensity of God's gifts there, our churches become catalysts of human flourishing: nurturing local economies and local culture, and seeking the common good of our places."[7] We must become people who listen to our communities better. This means we must also dwell, work, play, eat, and shop locally. By being present in these places more often, we become more aware of God's presence in our local communities.

We begin to address the needs of the community through observation: "The gospel becomes so much more tangible and compelling when the local church is actually a part of the community, connected to the struggles of the people and even the land itself."[8] Even taking the time to walk around the neighborhood can help the local church become more connected to the community. Walking helps us observe the space differently than driving or using public transit. While walking you can take notes on what you observe. Are there lots of children in the neighborhood? Are there none? Are the homes well-cared-for or not? Are people home during the day or at work? Where do people gather? Is there evidence of pets?

Walking and listening to your neighborhood helps connect congregants to the cycles and rhythms of the community. To take your observations more deeply, go for walks at various times of day and on different days of the week to see if your observations change. Taking notes and sharing them with the congregation can help discern as a community what God might be doing in the neighborhood and in what sort of ministry experiments the church could engage.

Moments of Silence

It might do us well to admit there are times when it feels like God is not listening or speaking. God feels distant, aloof, or as if God is intentionally ignoring us. We feel as though our prayers do not reach any further than the front of our own minds or the tips of our tongues. Just as biblical examples of God hearing and responding exist, there are also times when God intentionally does not hear or respond to the prayers and cries of God's people. God will not respond to the prayers of the oppressive, unjust, self-righteous, intentionally violent, or those who do not love others. In Amos 5:23-24 God tells the people through the prophet, "I will not listen to the melody of your harps. But let justice roll on like a river, and righteousness like a never-failing stream." Jesus teaches in his Sermon on the Mount, "Not everyone who says to me, 'Lord, Lord,' will enter the kingdom of heaven, but only the one who does the will of my Father who is in heaven" (Matthew 7:21). Jesus' brother James writes, "Look! The wages you failed to pay the workers who mowed your fields are crying out against you. The cries of the harvesters have reached the ears of the Lord Almighty" (James 5:4).

In times when we are made aware of our acts of sin toward others, we receive the opportunity to experience the grace of repentance. We can then work to redeem the damage done to others through our actions. To seek forgiveness and offer it in return are hallmarks of being a follower of Jesus.

We cannot place all the blame of God's silence on our sins. This would be woefully inadequate. Too many Christians journey through life faithfully following the ways of Christ only to be met with silence in the most difficult moments. Many saints before us have listened attentively to God's people and their communities only to feel the pain of loss and repeated disappointment in the midst of silence. Adam McHugh offers some wisdom in *The Listening Life* when he writes:

> I have found it comforting to think of God simply sitting with us in our pain, quietly listening. Maybe what feels like awkward and anxious silences to us are actually full and gentle silences. We are reminded that listening is not inaction. When God is listening to us, even if we do not experience the results we hope for, he is actively disposed toward us. We must remember that the fact that God hears prayers does not make him servile to our demands. Prayer words are not incantations with innate power to change divine weather patterns. When God doesn't give us our specific prayer requests, it may be an indication that he is working different things in us: things like trust, dependence, humility, patience, wisdom, even intimacy with him.
>
> . . . Even though we do not feel God's listening presence upon us, God is listening and silently working through our doubts and struggles. God may not be directly answering our prayers, but he is silently working though our lives, beckoning us closer, working new things into us.[9]

Even when we do not feel or clearly hear the presence of God we know God is silently working in us. God just might be working through grapevine conversations, neighborhood listening, or soul-filled silences.

Conclusion

To truly *shema* God and others requires something of us. It requires us to develop habits of listening to Scripture, other people, our neighborhoods, and experience. Listening is more than an auditory exercise. Listening is a deep practice of the soul. When we truly listen, we take our first steps at loving God and loving others. When we pay attention to the stories of God and the stories of others we can respond to them. Deep listening will not, and cannot, allow us to ignore what we have heard. If we *shema* we can respond to the words and actions of God by joining God in mission and ministry. If we *shema* others we will love them as God loves them.

Without listening we will never hear. If we never hear, we will never be moved to action. If we are never moved to action, we are missing our call to love God and to love others.

NOTES

1. Adam S. McHugh, *The Listening Life: Embracing Attentiveness in a World of Distraction* (Downers Grove, IL: InterVarsity Press, 2015), 16.
2. Dietrich Bonhoeffer, *Life Together* (New York: HarperCollins, 2005), 97.
3. Dan White, *Love Over Fear: Facing Monsters Befriending Enemies, and Healing Our Polarized World* (Chicago: Moody Publishers, 2019), 118.
4. C. Christopher Smith and John Pattison, *Slow Church: Cultivating Community in the Patient Way of Jesus* (Downers Grove, IL: InterVarsity Press, 2014), 43.
5. Paul Sparks, Tim Sorens, and Dwight J. Friesen, *The New Parish: How Neighborhood Churches Are Transforming Mission, Discipleship and Community* (Downers Grove, IL: InterVarsity Press, 2014), 23.
6. McHugh, *The Listening Life*, 51–52.
7. Smith and Pattison, *Slow Church*, 43.
8. Sparks, Sorens, and Friesen, *The New Parish*, 23.
9. McHugh, *The Listening Life*, 51–52.

5

Storytelling

"In the beginning," "Once upon a time," or even "In a galaxy far away" are all invitations to connect with a common story and the divine. Storytelling inhabits a powerful medium. No matter the content, one way or another, we are hearing about ourselves. Storytelling comes naturally to humans as we think in stories.[1] We are hard-wired to want to become part of stories that transform our lives. We have already discussed how to read the Bible as a narrative, allowing us to become participants in God's work in the world. We have also discussed the importance of listening to God and listening to others. Now comes the time when we need to take our turn and contribute to the conversation by sharing our story with others. Then we can become agents of transformation.

Stories Help Us Navigate Life

Being a person means having a story. Leonard Sweet states, "Every person is a story wrapped in skin. Moreover, everyone lives multistoried lives; as our lives intersect, so do our stories, and new stories splinter out from each encounter."[2] Inside of every story-carrying person lives a search for meaning. When people share their story, they navigate the big narrative questions of life based on their personal experiences and interpretations of those experiences. People ask "Who am I?" "What is going on here?" "What have I done?" and "Where am I going?" Without story we have no identity. Think of all the stories we have heard where people lose their memory. Our story helps us know and communicate our identities.

When people share their stories, they ask us to experience their lives with them. Storytellers invite listeners into their struggles, fears, and anxieties as well as their triumphs, loves, and moments of clarity. Our stories are rarely direct lines from point A to point B. Our stories, if told honestly, will reflect the twists and turns and complexity of our life experiences.

Our stories are holy. We may not use spiritual language when telling others about the disaster that was our fourth-grade talent show. We might not draw upon our theological vocabulary when referring to our traffic-filled workday commute. Yet, all of our stories are holy. In bearing God's image and participating in the world God created, they are holy. In expressing life, in one way or another, they are holy. When we tell our story, we speak of how we interpret the deeper meanings of life.

When I listen to others sharing their personal stories, I can often find myself in them. I identify with their struggles and victories. Their story brings to mind similar experiences I have had, and as the conversation moves forward I might share my story in turn to relate and connect with the person. Even if I cannot find my personal journey in their story, sometimes I can relate it to a universal experience. For example, I may not have ever experienced being fired from a job, but rejection comes as a common experience to all people. I do not know the joy of winning an athletic championship, but overcoming obstacles and achieving hard-won victories prevails as the plot of every underdog story.

We need well-told stories as stories help us understand and process our world. Stories also facilitate us making sense of our own lives. We need the stories of our neighbors, co-workers, families, friends, and church members. Coming from similar contexts, their stories may seem similar to ours. We can relate to them faster and more easily navigate their meaning. We also need stories that come from outside our immediate context to remind us of different experiences. Stories of hope, as well, encourage us to keep pursuing the good. We need to find ways to identify and participate in the unfolding foundational story of God at work in Jesus and the Holy Spirit everywhere in the world.

The Ultimate Story Told Around the Table

Our stories, as evidence of our search for meaning, carry holiness and significance. The ultimate story is the narrative of Scripture outlined earlier. It is about Jesus and what God has done in the past, does in the present, and will do in the future. It also connects each of us to one another and our Creator. Our stories intersect and interact with the ultimate story with each of our experiences. Our stories reveal our identity as much as they point to Christ and "[collapse] the distance between ourselves and the people who came before us, each one connecting ourselves to the people who will come after us . . . they point to the epic story of God and God's world; they are worth living and dying for."[3]

I believe the best place to tell a story is around a table laden with food and fellowship. The best stories I have ever heard I heard around tables. Holiday meals bring together families who retell the same stories year after year. Each year, with births, deaths, achievements, and disappointments, new stories are added to the tapestry of the family narrative. Business banquets pass on the stories of the trade, create and strengthen partnerships, and celebrate successes. Lunch with a neighbor or friend strengthens relationships, passes on the heritage of the community, and opens the door to deeper connections. Snacks with children make the imagination run wild and create space for them to ask questions about life.

There is something powerful about gathering around a table to share a story. It is almost primal. Instinctively, no matter our culture, we feel the urge to share ourselves and learn more about those at the table. We crave the presence of others at meal times. Some restaurants have even begun to create space for solo diners to gather together with others.

My wife and I enjoy going out for dinner on occasion. About once or twice a year, we splurge and go to a local hibachi grill. For those who may not know, a hibachi grill is Asian cuisine prepared in front of you. When you enter a hibachi-style restaurant, you usually sit at a table with six to eight strangers all facing the grill. Each person chooses an entrée, but the sides are common to all. The knife-wielding, spatula-twirling chef prepares the rice and vegetables and various meats while making bad jokes about the ingredients. It is all rather symbolic. We all share common food while still having unique aspects to our meal. While the food cooks, we like to meet the people around the table with whom we share rice and vegetables. Inevitably, people start to share stories around the time salads are served, and for the next hour or so we receive glimpses into the souls of our fellow diners. We can see the work of God in each person and each story. It encourages me to learn how God moves in my neighborhood by listening to my fellow diners share even the smallest sliver of their life around a grill. It is also always comical to watch people try to catch flying shrimp with open mouths like a bunch of trained seals.

Telling stories around dinner tables is far more natural than sharing stories on a plane, in line at the DMV, or in the hospital waiting room. Yes, great stories can be shared in these and many other spaces, but it has been my experience that the best stories are told around tables.

Jesus told some of his best stories around tables filled with people of ill repute and holy rollers alike. He gathered around tables to tell stories so often he was accused of being a drunkard and a friend of sinners. "The kingdom of heaven is like . . . ," "A certain man was preparing a banquet and invited many guests . . . ," "Suppose a woman had ten silver coins and loses one . . . ," "A man had two sons . . . ," "A man of noble birth . . . gave his servants ten minas . . . ," "This is my body" and "This is my blood" all introduced stories Jesus told while sitting around tables. He shared stories about the kingdom of God between the salad and lamb servings. His stories forced listeners to examine themselves between scoops of sweet figs and honey-covered apples. Some of his stories were even about food, banquets, and hospitality. The stories Jesus told changed the world so profoundly we keep retelling them around our personal dinner tables and the communion table on Sunday mornings.

My dad is an excellent storyteller. As retired military, he spent much of his life in the air looking over the various landscapes of the world as he has standing on it. He has been to every continent and nearly one hundred countries. He can't even tell you about some of his adventures (or so he claims . . . a master stroke of storyteller intrigue). Now a high school JROTC (Junior Reserve Officer Training Corps) instructor and social studies/geography teacher, he has a six-foot-wide map of the world in his classroom with pins pressed into all the places he has visited. Just point to one and ask, "When did you go to . . ." and he will regale you with a tale of mythic proportions.

His best stories come at the end of a big meal. With a captive audience waiting for dessert or the check, he will launch into adventures about a time when a plane he was flying started to fall apart at twenty-five thousand feet and how they salvaged the wing using duct tape and glue; or how one time he and some friends went to visit the local village in South America and ended up singing songs all night with a family of poncho weavers; or he might tell you about the time he played golf at three in the morning in broad daylight in Alaska but got lost on the fourteenth hole and had to ride a reindeer back to the barracks; or how after a major surgery he sneaked out of bed one night with IV lines still attached, wearing a gown that didn't close in the back, and taught the entire ICU nursing staff the Macarena. At this point I am not sure how much is midrash and how much is true, but his stories are always entertaining. They always reveal a little of his love for adventure, a little of his personality, and a lot about a God who watches over fools.

Have you ever been at dinner table with a pastor? If you have, then you know a pastor always has a story to tell and cannot tell just a short story. Some of the best storytellers I know are pastors. These gifted men and women can turn a five-minute shopping experience at the local grocer into a thirty-minute epic adventure full of drama and laughter. They will delight you with stories of baptisms gone awry, sermonic blunders, comical visitations, academic training, and professional struggles. They carry on about books, conferences, fishing outings, youthful rebellion, and a mischievous middle age. They will also share about the power of redemption, restorations, and reconciliation in their own lives and the lives of their parishioners.

When I sit at a table with a good storyteller, and after I wipe the tears from my eyes and rub my cheeks from so much laughter, I come to realize their stories are all similar. The characters, settings, and time periods shift, but they share similar qualities. The stories told at a local hibachi, my father's dinner table, or a pastors' conference, the stories shared in your local coffee diner, bookshop, movie theater, Netflix queue, or dining room are all the same. Ultimately, these stories help us know who we are, where we come from, where we are going, what we care about, and a God present in and through it all.

Perhaps the author of Ecclesiastes was correct; maybe "there is nothing new under the sun" (Ecclesiastes 1:9). When we gather around the table we share similar stories. Perhaps you have a basic set of stories you feel comfortable sharing that help give people a sense of your identity. Maybe your culture informs the type of stories appropriate for sharing. Whatever story you are willing to share is important. It tells, at least in part, the winding path that led to the table that you now share with others. It is a holy story, whether we use religious language or not. It describes our interaction with the divine and our search for meaning. They are significant and holy because your story is our story.

A Brilliant Short Story

The best stories hold a mirror up to the reader or listener. They force readers or listeners to ask questions about who they are and what they believe. The story of Jonah, for example, brilliantly communicates a Jewish prophet's struggle to submit to God as well as Israel as a light to the nations. The story also focuses on the consistency of the character of God, even when we wish God acted differently. It is about hearing the call to repent and responding with humility. It is about being stubborn and selfish. It is about being angry at God. It is about prejudice and mercy. In short it is about us. This short story powerfully shares my story, your story, God's story, and the corporate story of humanity.

The unique story of Jonah, unlike books attributed to other minor prophets, tells about Jonah. All the other prophetic books in the Hebrew Bible instead primarily share the messages the prophets delivered. There is little in those stories to tell us about the character, personality, and beliefs of the prophets themselves. The other prophetic stories are all told from a perspective of obedience as those prophets generally follow the leading of the Spirit in word and deed. The story of Jonah is very different. It is more like the stories of Elijah, Elisha, Ruth, Esther, or the first half of Daniel. You see a character interacting with God and people, revealing their good and bad qualities.

Jonah, a prophet from northern Israel, receives a command to travel to the Assyrian city of Nineveh and preach against the wickedness that has corrupted the great city. God judges the darkness shrouding the city and wants to give the people a chance to respond to the light. A good short story makes connections to other stories by providing necessary background without having to elaborate on them. Here, informational reading of the Bible meets formational reading. Genesis 10:8-10 tells us that Nimrod, one of the great-grandsons of Noah and a hunter of man and beast, created Nineveh and Babylon. Together, Babylon and Nineveh serve as the ultimate examples of humanity's fall into chaos and violence throughout the biblical narrative.

Good stories are typically also contextually relevant. The first introduction of Jonah in 2 Kings 14 illustrates him as a shady advisor to the tyrannical king Jeroboam II and a member of a group of zealous Israelites who want to prevent Assyria from invading again by building a northern border wall. Israel often fell victim to the power of Assyria and its capital, Nineveh, a "city of blood, full of lies, full of plunder, never without victims . . . who enslaved nations" (Nahum 3:1, 4). God wants Jonah, a shady prophet to a ironhanded king, to cease his zealous defense of Israel's nationalism by building a wall. Furthermore, God asks Jonah to sheath his sword and put his construction equipment back in the shed. The call is to go and *be with* the Ninevites. God wants to show compassion and mercy on a people who have repeatedly caused great harm and violence on the people of Israel. For all his faults, Jonah knows God's character, and that is revealed in God's request for him to go to Nineveh.

Instead of following the steps of other prophets, Jonah runs away, leading the reader to feel immediately on-guard about what comes next in this story. As modern readers we might not immediately understand why Jonah runs; that will come later. Fellow Israelite nationalists who first heard this story might have seen Jonah as a hero and may have responded like Jonah if called to Nineveh. Jonah flees to Israel's best harbor, Joppa, and finds the first ship headed southwest, in the opposite direction of Nineveh.

Jonah promptly goes below deck and attempts to sleep away his worries. Meanwhile, above deck a storm begins to rage. The chaotic waters of Genesis come to mind. The sailors try to rescue the ship by throwing the cargo overboard and praying. When this fails to solve the problem, they throw dice and accuse Jonah as the culprit behind the divine weather pattern. The sailors want to know who Jonah is, where he is from, and what he has done to incur such a response from God. Jonah confesses, "I am a Hebrew and I worship the LORD, the God of heaven, who made the sea and the dry land" (Jonah 1:9). Jonah asks the crew to throw him overboard.

This might sound noble, but, through his willingness to place his death on the shoulders of the sailors, Jonah exhibits selfishness. If the sailors, who now fear God and this storm, throw Jonah overboard, what might God do to them if they engage in homicide? In the ancient world, you could not murder someone without a trial, any more than today. If they kill

Jonah without a trial, one of Jonah's relatives might have a right to kill the sailors in return as blood-guilt. So, to avoid trial or death, the sailors strive all the harder to get back to land. After further efforts to bring the vessel safely to shore fail, the sailors cry out to the Lord for mercy as they throw Jonah over the side with the other cargo. The winds cease, and the sea grows calm. The sailors offer a sacrifice to the Lord and make vows to God.

Good storytelling will use tropes and stereotypes and turn them on their ear for effect. The sailors clearly served other gods besides the Hebrew God, YHWH, demonstrated by their cries out to them when the storm first began. They are possibly Canaanites, Philistines, or other coastal people at odds with Israel. Instead of portraying the sailors as vengeful, violent, or dimwitted, the writer depicts them as helpful, kind, and wise enough to discern that their prophetic passenger played a part in the storm. This might be our first clue as to how God viewed the people of Nineveh as well. The sailors have a dramatic conversion experience. Jonah, despite his best efforts to be a terrible prophet, unintentionally aided in the conversion of a sailing crew. This reveals God's character as gracious and merciful on the crew even when Jonah is not.

God summons a huge fish to consume Jonah, but in God's mercy the fish does not destroy Jonah. Instead, Jonah's time inside the fish becomes a dark and slimy three-day submarine trip back to land. The poem in Jonah 2 offers a moment for Jonah to reflect on his relationship with God. In his darkest moment, he cries out to God and is rescued from the depths of the sea. But he doesn't repent in the poem. In fact, Jonah seems to double down on his belief that God has nothing but wrath in store for those unlike himself. He is right that "salvation comes from the LORD" (Jonah 2:9), but he is wrong in believing it is only for Israel.

On the third day, the fish vomits Jonah back onto dry ground. Jonah travels inland toward Nineveh. When he finally arrives, Jonah provides a bare minimum sermon for the people of Nineveh. He walks into a town square and proclaims, "Forty more days and Nineveh will be overthrown" (Jonah 3:4). In the Hebrew, the sermon contains five words. After that Jonah leaves, climbs a nearby hill, and waits for the city to catch fire. Only it never does.

The people of Nineveh are so moved by the proclamation of destruction they humble themselves by declaring a fast and putting on sackcloth as signs of contrition. The king of Nineveh hears about the sermon and fasts and humbles himself as well. He calls on all the Ninevites to give up their evil ways and violence because, "Who knows? God may yet relent and with compassion turn from his fierce anger so that we will not perish" (Jonah 3:9). The most powerful character presented so far, a king, is humbled to the point of repentance, and, in a moment of comic relief, calls on all the animals to repent as well.

God's character is again revealed as merciful and compassionate. God *shemas* the people of Nineveh's prayers of repentance and relents from the prophesied destruction. This news reaches the ears of Jonah up on the hill overlooking the city, and it makes him angry. We finally learn that Jonah did not want to go to Nineveh, knowing God expresses gracious compassion and is known to withhold calamity on those who in our human judgments seem to deserve it most. Here, Jonah reveals his motives. Jonah, a devoted Israelite nationalist, harbored anger and hostility toward the nations to whom God asked him to bring light. He decides he will never relinquish his hatred of the Assyrians and especially those in Nineveh for their past atrocities. He demonstrates his stubbornness, self-righteousness, and bad-tempered qualities by rejecting

God's mercy to the people of Nineveh, who are regularly seen as the epitome of human rebellion in the narrative of Israel.

The remainder of Jonah 4 deepens this point. A plant grows overnight and gives shade to Jonah. He rejoices and expresses gratitude. The next day a worm consumes the plant, killing it just as quickly as it grew. Jonah gets so angry that, for the third time in the story, he wishes to die. Jonah would rather die than live in a world where Ninevites receive God's love and mercy. God asks if he has any right to be angry. Should God not have mercy on a massive city so blinded by evil?

The story ends leaving us with many questions. Do we accept the mercy of God on our lives while denying the mercy of God on the lives of others? Are we okay with God loving our enemies as much as God loves us? Do we place our national allegiance over against the grace of God on the world? Do we run from God's call on our lives if we don't like God? Do we need to reevaluate our understanding of God considering God's consistent grace seen in the story? Am I most like Jonah, the sailors, the Ninevites, the king, or the penitent animals? What hostilities and prejudices do we carry that need to be released?

This is a great story. It contains land and sea adventures, a giant monster fish, a tiny plant-eating worm, wave-crashing storms, and scorching dry heat. It also discusses isolation, companionship, suicide by sailing crew, merciful forgiveness, and political and social intrigue. The supposed villains become repentant followers of God, and the hero turns out to be a bit of a hard-hearted villain. The story, it turns out, is not about Jonah or the sailors or even the Ninevites—it is about a mercifully consistent God who righteously judges evil but always offers one more chance at restoration and reconciliation. The power of this short story (only 1,082 words in Hebrew) shines through its relatable characters, introspection, and call for the reader to wrestle with the identity of God. A good story contains all this, and our personal stories can do this too if we share them with honesty.

Telling Your Story

Living a table life includes sharing your story with others, especially your church community and neighborhood. Although important and significant, storytelling does not need to be complicated. The story of Jonah, for example, holds many layers and meaning, but it is not a complicated story. You could probably memorize it verbatim with enough practice. When you begin to think about how you want to craft your personal story, consider what this time will mean for you and your faith community. This is an opportunity for you to share honestly who you are with others. Storytelling allows your fellow followers of Jesus and neighbors to know you. That is scary business filled with risk and vulnerability. By sharing your story with others, you invite them to become part of your ongoing story.

When you gather around the table to share your story you want to honor the time of those gathered together. I suggest preparing your narrative in advance of the gathering. By preparing your narrative in advance you will be able to choose pieces of your story that best communicate how you have come to be at this table. Choose stories that communicate who you are as a person. This might include your passions, interests, hobbies, and basic family dynamics. You might also choose to include times of struggle, setbacks, and doubts. Are there key life moments worth sharing, like graduations, marriages, births or deaths, vocational accomplishments, or baptism? Have there been seasons of spiritual awakening or seasons filled with long dark nights of the soul?

Learning to create a personal narrative is simple to do even if it requires a little practice. Using guiding questions and statements can help you begin to formulate your personal narrative: "Where did you grow up?" "Describe your job or vocation." "Where do you see God working in your life right now?" "What have been some of the most life-giving experiences in your life?"[4]

As you work through these questions and ponder how you might share your story with others, keep in mind that living a table life means honoring people's presence. I recommend keeping your personal narrative under twenty to twenty-five minutes. If you are in community with them long-term, there will be other times to share more in the future.

When it is time to share your story, do so in a comfortable setting with limited distractions. A dinner table offers a good space for sharing. Other good spaces include a living room, deck, or patio with adequate seating. I know of one group who met in their church, which provided enough room for everyone. Place the storyteller in a position where that person can be seen and heard easily.

The moment of storytelling can be as formal or informal as necessary for the comfort of the group. It is a good idea for the storytellers to determine the dynamics of their presentation, allowing the person to feel as comfortable as possible when sharing. Some groups might choose to place their storyteller in the front to present to the group. Other groups might be more casual and simply sit to share. Some storytellers want the group to remain silent until they are done sharing. Still other storytellers prefer to welcome questions and positive comments along the way from the gathered community.

As a listener, be prepared to learn new things about your Christian brothers and sisters. When they finish sharing, be ready to affirm their courage to share with the group. If they feel comfortable, have the group lay hands on them and pray for them, thanking God for their story. This is one of the most vulnerable moments in the life of a person. How a group responds to the storyteller will have lasting impacts on how the person feels received by the community. It can do lasting damage to a person who feels the community has rejected or diminished their story when hoping for acceptance.

As a storyteller, be prepared to experience what my close friend calls "an emotional hangover." Preparing and sharing your story can emotionally and spiritually drain you. It takes courage to be vulnerable with others. It requires us to face certain truths within ourselves and ask difficult questions of identity. It requires us to examine God's presence in our lives and the world around us. It might cause us to ask new questions that will require deep prayer and reflection. However, the experience of sharing your story with others will lead to affirmation and love and a deeper connection to those you share with.

Not everybody feels comfortable with speaking in public. For some, just reading this chapter makes their hearts pound and palms sweat. Some people are naturally private persons and do not wish to share their life story with others. They have spent their entire life building safety walls around their personal space. For others it takes time to get to know people well to trust them. It might take more than three meals before they feel able to share their lives with others. All of this is normal and okay.

Storytelling is a spiritual habit important to practice in a community. I would challenge and encourage anyone hesitant to share their story to consider ways in which they might be comfortable communicating. Perhaps an introverted or private person might be one of the last people in the group to share in order to gauge how open other people are and honor their openness by sharing some. Perhaps they might share in small doses, sharing simple truths about themselves over the course of several meetings. A private person or a person slow to trust might host a meal in a place that gives them comfort, strength, and courage and channel that safety into feeling ready to share their personal narratives.

Community requires all of us to give and to receive. If you are part of a group where the other members openly share their lives, their homes, their joys, and their doubts, it is important to reciprocate as much as possible. This does not mean everyone must share at the same level. Some people actively share all their dirty laundry without looking back. But most of us are not that open. It takes time and it takes trust. Putting yourself before your community places you in a vulnerable and risk-filled position. If people trust you with their story, do your best to share as much of your story as you can with them in return. I commend your courage in participating in this challenging spiritual habit.

Beyond the Personal Narrative

When living a table life you may arrive at a place where everyone has shared their personal narrative. At this point in the process, some groups change the construction of their meetings. A congregation might consider bringing an end to a round of table groups and re-create new groups, allowing each person in the congregation an opportunity to be in table life with as many other congregants as possible. If this occurs, it is a good idea to repeat the process and have people share their narratives again with the new group. This will help people continue to grow close to the entire congregation.

If, however, a table group continues to meet after everyone has shared their personal narrative, you might want to try open-ended questions for the entire group to answer. Use simple questions to guide the conversation for the group such as: "What Gospel passage do you most resonate with?" "Where did you see God at work in your family this week?"

"Where might the Spirit be leading our church community?"[5] Provide a list of questions centered around past, present, and future conversation topics covering where you see God at work throughout your life.

These types of open-ended questions allow everyone in the table group to share their response to the questions for a few moments. These questions help facilitate group conversation as opposed to the previous personal narrative monologue. The first few times you begin your conversations with these types of questions it might begin with awkward silences. Do not feel pressured to fill the space with unnecessary comments. Trust the Spirit to fill the space as the Spirit did on Mount Horeb for Elijah. Once people begin sharing their observations from their engagement with the Spirit, be encouraging of their reflections. As more people share, you may discover that people have similar experiences. This could be a sign of where Christ is leading the congregation.

Being part of a continuous small group within a larger community increases the depth of relationships. The cumulative effect of multiple conversations and meals together impacts the group like a river slowly carving the landscape. There are moments of mighty torrents where you may discover new ground, but mostly it is a slow, unyielding process of mature growth. I have been privileged to work in contexts where I can take regular lunch breaks with the same person over long periods of time. For five years I met with my friend Tom when I was new to pastoral ministry, and for the past eight years, I have met with my friend Robin. Just about every workday for the past thirteen years has been spent in the company of one of these men. There have indeed been watershed moments, but mostly we have consistently connected with one another and the work of Christ in our midst. These conversations have shaped me in powerful ways.

Table Life Covenant

Table life is most effective when people feel comfortable with their table group. By creating a covenantal agreement it encourages participants to be present at all gatherings, to participate openly and honestly in the conversations and meals, and to maintain a level of confidentiality that helps everyone in the group exhibit higher levels of trust and engagement. A covenant agreement does not set out to define the ideal group. We already learned from Dietrich Bonhoeffer that anyone in pursuit of the ideal Christian community is set up for failure. Instead, a covenant agreement outlines what the individuals within the group are willing to do to strengthen the table life experience for everyone involved.

Having these table life groups adhere to a series of agreements allows everyone to understand their commitment and encourages them to honor their agreement. A good covenant should include things that demonstrate your desire to honor the time set aside and the other people involved in the fellowship meals. It sets out to define the beginning and the end of the process. This way everyone involved is aware of the length of their commitment. It states a willingness to love the table life members as you learn new aspects of their lives and personalities. It challenges you to remain faithful to the process, knowing at some point it would be easier to just skip a gathering or stop attending.

Guiding people into intentional intimate fellowship has provided spiritual directors and retreat centers key insights into how to shape and guide small groups similar to those encouraged in table life. Many of them recommend having participants in any small group context adhere to a covenant agreement. Here is a sample covenant agreement I have adapted from Dr. Jeff Savage's work with small groups in his congregation and spiritual direction courses.[6]

Sample Table Life Covenant

In utter dependence upon Jesus Christ as my Savior, Teacher, Lord, and Table Host I will seek continual renewal through spiritual practices of table life, exercise of my spiritual gifts, and participation in acts of service. In addition:

I will meet with my table life group [write out the frequency, such as the third Thursday of the month], because I know my participation is crucial to our table life continuity.

I promise to keep whatever is shared within the confines of this group.

I will come prepared to dwell in the Word and share my insights, listen to Scripture and my fellow table life participants, and share my personal narrative in return.

I will participate in planned group meals and share in communion.

I promise to love my table life brothers and sisters faithfully, no matter what their past contains or what happens in their present lives. I will attempt to love each one as a child of God and do all I can to express God's faithful love.

I promise to regularly pray for each member of my table life group.

I agree to communicate my true opinions, feelings, struggles, and joys.

I will be sensitive to the table life group's needs to the best of my ability, as I trust the table life group will be to me. I will try to hear them, see their point of view, and understand their feelings.

Believing in the importance of commitment, I will do my best to remain actively involved through the entire commitment period. Should I wish to exit the group, I will discuss this with the whole group at least fourteen days in advance.

This covenant begins [date] and continues until [date], at which time decisions about current and new table life groups will be made.

Signed: ______________________ Date: ______________________

Conclusion

Your story is holy. It is the chronicle of your life. It is a narrative of God's interactive presence in the world in general and your life in particular. We might not use spiritual language when we share our stories with others, but our stories are nonetheless holy retellings of our experiences. Our stories do not have to be dramatic. They do not have to be filled with peaks and valleys. Stories do not always need to be framed in the context of "my life was like A before I became a Christian but now it is like B since becoming a Christian." These are not bad outlines, but they are not the only outlines available.

A quick survey of the Bible will reveal many characters who struggle with faith and life. Few characters always got it right. That is why we relate to them so well. Each of our individual stories offers a mini-retelling of the human condition and our search for meaning. As we share our stories, we seek to be known, understood, and loved. As we listen to the stories of others, we become part of their story.

When we become part of each other's stories we become a community. Worship services, Sunday school classes, and midweek Bible studies are important aspects of our faith journeys; however, they do not provide a space to share our larger stories. Living a table life invites us to create space to share intentionally our stories with others. This is why we learn so much more about our fellow congregants on a week-long mission trip than we do the other fifty-one weeks in the year. It is about creating space to tell stories and share our lives with others. If we want to grow a stronger community, we need to create spaces where people tell their stories to one another.

NOTES

1. William J. Bausch, *Storytelling: Imagination and Faith* (Mystic, CT: Twenty-Third Publications, 1984), 9.
2. Leonard I. Sweet, *From Talent to Table: Where Community Is Found and Identity is Formed* (Colorado Springs, CO: NavPress, 2014), 33.
3. Sweet, *From Tablet to Table*, 35.
4. For a list of starting questions to help formulate your personal narrative, see Appendix B.
5. For a fuller list of potential sharing questions, see Appendix C.
6. Used with permission from Dr. Jeff Savage, First Baptist Church, Springfield, Oregon.

6
Communion

Russian iconographer Andrei Rublev is considered one of the world's most important artists of the fifteenth century. Not much about the life and career of Rublev is certain. Scholars believe he was born sometime between 1360 and 1370. We know he, as a junior apprentice, joined a team of artists commissioned to paint icons and frescos for the Cathedral of Annunciation on the Kremlin Square in Moscow in 1405. For the next twenty-five years, Rublev spent his time in the sanctuaries, halls, and basements of churches across Russia painting icons of Christ, Mary, the apostles, saints, heaven, and various biblical scenes to guide parishioners in worship. Rublev died at the Andronikov Monastery in 1430, leaving a legacy of some of the most important medieval Byzantium icons in the world. His influence on Eastern Orthodoxy and Russian culture made such an impact that the Russian Orthodox Church canonized Rublev as a saint in 1988 and celebrates his feast day every January 29.

Rublev spent a lifetime trying to capture the narrative of Scripture in works of visual art during a time when most people did not read well and had limited access to the written Scriptures, but could readily engage with Scripture through acts of worship, habits of discipleship, and reflection on art. To this day hundreds of icons fill Russian Orthodox church walls, reminding worshipers of the saints living before them, church history, and images of the biblical narrative. Eastern Orthodox icons, in particular, communicate vast symbolism. Colors, clothing, halos, hand gestures, facial expressions, and numbers all contain specific meanings that help the viewer see the spiritual depth of these icons.

Rublev's most famous painting is called *The Trinity*. Created sometime between 1425 and 1427, Trinity Cathedral actively used it in worship as part of the iconostasis; however, the painting was moved to Tretyakov Gallery in Moscow in 1929. The icon stands almost five feet tall and four feet wide. The vertically aligned wooden panels feature three angels sitting around a modest table set with only a single cup. The icon reinterprets Genesis 18 where three angels visit Abraham near his tent by the trees of Mamre. In the painting, a house and tree sit in the background, but the angelic beings gathered around the table act as the center of the entire painting.

More can be said about the angels than first appearance. Gathered around the table, they form a circle of communal welcome. Expressed through their turned position, the eyes of the angels seem to defer to one another. Each captures a unique quality, yet is equal to the other two. Their iconic colorful robes tell of their angelic character. The portrayal of their age, all identical, also symbolizes the Trinity. Gold represents the radiance of heaven, perfection, and the Father; green represents new life, new creation, and the Holy Spirit; red represents divine life while blue represents human life; and the Son, shrouded in both, illustrates God made flesh and dwelling among creation. The Jesus figure blesses the cup with a raised hand. The Holy Trinity sits at a table with a blessed cup in a state of perpetual divine invitation. They sit with one side of the table eternally open, welcoming every person who looks upon the icon into communion and fellowship.

I have been deeply touched by this classic work of art. Each time I look at Rublev's *The Trinity* I am reminded again that I am always welcome at the table. When I find myself rudderless or disoriented by life, I sit before *The Trinity* to regain my bearings. When feelings of loneliness or isolation creep into my soul, the presence of this image in my office and in my home reminds me that the Father, Son, and Holy Spirit, in perpetual communion with one another, host a table where I and all those around me are welcome. *The Trinity* is a work of art larger than itself that embodies Christ's invitation to communion with him.

Take, Bless, Break, and Give

Throughout the Gospels, Jesus sits at tables. No matter if he sits on a grassy hillside, in a Pharisee's rural home, in the dining room of a tax collector, on a rocky lakeshore, or in a locked room, Jesus always manages to host the meal. In meals where Jesus is present, he always takes, blesses (or gives thanks), breaks, and gives the bread to those gathered. This pattern is seen repeatedly in the Gospels. These verbs appear in this order in the feeding of the four thousand (Mark 8:6; Matthew 14:13-21), five thousand (Matthew 14:19-20; Mark 6:41; John 6:11), and at the Last Supper (Mark 14:22-24). They are seen again with the dinner along the Emmaus Road (Luke 24:30-31). Paul, extending this pattern beyond the Gospels, uses these verbs when he explains how Christian dinners work to the Corinthians (1 Corinthians 11:23-26). The words "taking," "blessing," "breaking," and "giving" express what Jesus did, and retell the story of Jesus. Since we gather at the table in remembrance of him, we do it as he did it.

When we gather around the table for communion in remembrance of Jesus, we bring ourselves, in addition to the necessary materials, to the table. Bread and juice, plates and cups, wood and glass and metals are all summoned. We are like the boy who brings his loaves and fishes wrapped in a well-worn cloth, the disciples who offer their catch in nets woven by their own hands, or, like Matthew or Zacchaeus, who can afford to purchase the finest china in town. This is our offering. We bring our earthly wares and our human selves to the table: "We offer and he takes. He refuses nothing of who we are, what we have done . . . God does not exploit us; God does not force us. He takes only what we offer."[1]

Jesus takes what we offer him—ourselves and our foods—and blesses them. We bring our stuff and ourselves in hopes that he will bless our offerings and return them changed through the work of Christ. The word *blessed* implies that a divine being has somehow bestowed something upon us. God receives our breads, our cups, and our very selves out of love and blessing for God's creation. Jesus may have offered the classic Hebrew meal blessing: "Blessed are you, Lord our God, King of the universe, who brings forth bread from the earth." It is with such prayers and blessings that we are reminded of God's intentionality and purpose in creation. Everything, from the simple to the ordinary to the material, finds goodness in God.[2]

When participating in communion, I regularly examine my life as 1 Corinthians 11:28 encourages. I also give thanks. During the Eucharist, which means thanksgiving, I give thanks for those who gather at the table with me as well as for Christ's invitation for us all to come together as a community to his table. The welcoming nature of the table that repeats the story of Christ's redeeming acts overwhelms me with gratitude, perhaps even more so knowing that this redemption does not include only me, but the whole of creation.

Jesus does not stop at blessing. He breaks the bread. Our sacrificial gifts of food and self do not remain the same after they have entered the hands of Jesus. The breaking of bread, on a practical level, functions as a method of distribution just as we smash grapes into juice to share with others. But when Jesus breaks bread and pours cups they always multiply. Bread cannot multiply unless it is broken. Jesus himself is the one who was broken, and his sacrifice was enough for all of creation—past, present, and future. When we come to the table, we should expect also to be broken in some way: "In our *brokenness,* we are *beloved.* In our frailty, God remains faithful."[3] The breaking of our pride, self-sufficiency, and self-loathing opens us to new life.[4] Everything brought to the table is shared and broken for the purpose of Christ. That way, everything brought to the table—food, material goods, and people—"will flow forth from the table through the whole of our lives and then return all over again."[5] Experiencing brokenness dismantles the myth of salvation as a self-help program. Brokenness is the process by which Jesus reshapes our food and us for the purpose of his kingdom.

After taking, blessing, and breaking the meal, Jesus gives it all back anew. "Jesus gives back what we bring him, who we are; and we receive what he gives. But it is no longer what we brought. It has been changed into what God gives . . . everything we give to Jesus is given back, but lavishly."[6] A few loaves and fishes become leftovers after feeding thousands. A few spiritually ragged and emotionally raw disciples preaching on Pentecost become the foundation of the global movement two thousand years in the making. The single sacrifice of Jesus becomes the final, all-sufficient sacrifice for all of creation.

When we gather at the table and experience taking, blessing, and breaking, Jesus then ushers us out into the world. God wants more for us than to just receive the kingdom: we are to participate in the coming reign of King Jesus by joining in his mission.

> As ones who have received His grace and have been put right, we are signs of a new creation in the world (see 2 Corinthians 5:17). As ones who work in the Lord so that the work of the Lord will continue, we are agents of the new creation arriving even now (see 1 Corinthians 15:58) . . . It takes a big view of the gospel to see this truth . . . The mission of God has always been on track. And the mode of that mission has always been human beings, God's image bearers and mission carriers.[7]

We go just as we are—taken, blessed, broken, and given by Christ himself.

Jesus Extends a Table Invitation to All

Why are there so many verses in the Bible about listening, love, unity, and holiness? Could the reason be that listening, loving, communing, and seeking holiness are vital to our roles as Christians? Could the reason also include the necessary reminder for us to know the true meaning of these acts? Are we so shaped by division and hostility that we constantly need our imaginations reshaped by the possibility of unity and holiness?

Community functions as one of the most important themes in Scripture. From the beginning, God recognizes Adam's need for a companion. God promises Abraham that he will have descendants so numerous they cannot be counted. Those descendants become the nation of Israel, who are called to observe the Torah as a community. The earliest followers of Jesus form clusters of fellowship that observe the teaching of the apostles, share community, break bread, and pray together. The new heaven and new earth will be filled with the presence of God, Son, and Holy Spirit in perfect fellowship with one another and with all the people of God.

Living into the kingdom narrative of Jesus requires a community of fellowship. No single person can hope to fully embody the narrative alone. Participation with other Jesus followers in the context of a church community is a crucial part of the Christian experience. This has always been the case. We need one another. Jesus said all who come to his table of fellowship and follow his kingdom narrative are brothers and sisters (Mark 3:34-35). With God as our Father, Christ as our Savior, and the Holy Spirit as the one who unites us, we are a family—the people of God.

Yet, we have an open secret we do not always like to admit: being in community with other followers of Jesus is difficult and messy. Every community that seeks to be in peaceful harmony with one another knows this truth. In January 2013, N. T. Wright addressed the Scottish Church Society Conference on the book of Ephesians. In that address he said:

> I have come to the preliminary conclusion that the central symbol of Paul's worldview is the Church itself, precisely in its unity and in its holiness. On the street, what the onlooker is supposed to see is a community that is united and a community that dances to a different drummer, that does stuff differently . . . Pastors will know that it is easy to have either unity or holiness in the Church, but hard to get both at the same time! Paul insists on both.[8]

I have worked with multiple congregations over the years that have experienced some level of community conflict. Conflict in churches runs the gambit. There are staffing issues, building maintenance, interpersonal conflicts between congregants, missional direction, theological debates, financial struggles, ethical conundrums, racial divides, leadership power plays, and many more. Being in a community with other followers of Jesus does not guarantee people will be of one heart and mind. When individuals, congregations, and denominations diligently exercise habits of discipleship and common-sense practices that allow them to be more prepared to follow the Sprit, they can then embody Ephesians 4:1-6.

The hard, honest truth that church communities come with challenges and messes exists because we seek Jesus in these very places. The Christian church is not like any other social experience. The messiness of church arises when we seek to bring in our personal expectations that have little to do with the Christian experience. Many of us search for an ideal community that meets our perceived needs, are filled with people who agree with us, and perfectly align with our theological conclusions.

Twentieth-century British author C. S. Lewis wrote a fictional tale about a demon in training called *The Screwtape Letters*. In this story, the demon named Screwtape mentors his nephew, Woomword, to tempt a British man, simply known as the Patient, away from God. Wormwood observes the habits and nature of humanity and learns all the basic temptations of human folly. In a collection of thirty-one letters written by Screwtape, you discover Wormwood has trouble keeping the man away from developing a closer relationship with God. Along the way the man becomes a Christian and begins to go to church. Wormwood seems powerless to stop the man from attending church and engaging in community.

Uncle Screwtape provides advice on how to better tempt the man away from a life in Christian community in letter 16:

> Surely you know that if a man can't be cured of church-going, the next best thing is to send him all over the

> neighborhood looking for the church that "suits" him until he becomes a taster or connoisseur of churches.
>
> The reasons are obvious. In the first place the parochial organization should always be attacked, because, being a unity of place and not of likings, it brings people of different classes and psychology together in the kind of unity the Enemy desires . . . In the second place, the search for a "suitable" church makes the man a critic.[9]

Regular participation in communion with our fellow believers in Christ helps us avoid becoming "connoisseurs" and "critics" who disrupt community. Regular participation in communion dismantles the belief of church as a solitary place. Gathering with other people who bring their messy lives to the table where Jesus acts as host will shatter any notions that the ideal Christian community is one free from messiness. The unity and holiness described in the New Testament are not givens, but rather attained through intentional communal striving.

Twentieth-century German theologian Dietrich Bonhoeffer puts it like this: "By sheer grace, God will not permit us to live even for a brief period in a dream world . . . Only that fellowship which faces such disillusionment, with all its unhappy and ugly aspects, begins to be what it should be in God's sight, begins to grasp in faith the promise that is given to it."[10]

If the community called church is to deal adequately with the messiness of a life, and seek to live a kingdom narrative different from the ones given to us by others, we must be able to admit that it requires challenging work. There is no room for pursuing easily attained dream worlds. Genuine community includes some unhappy and ugly aspects in its pursuit of unity and holiness.

Unity and holiness are attainable, however. Unity requires us to be shaped by the communion table and have difficult conversations about the many narratives that compete for primacy in our lives. This includes conversations about racial reconciliation, economic oppression, gender equality, political ideologies, sexual identities, and every other difficult issue. The conversations around the table are not limited to large-scale systemic issues alone. Interpersonal grievances and differences must also be addressed: whom have I lied to, whose trust have I broken, what commitments have I failed to uphold, and other covenantal failures. The communion table creates the space necessary for us to confess to Christ and to one another the ways in which we have sinned and injured. The communion table molds us into people capable of giving and receiving forgiveness and who pursue genuine reconciliation in all our relationships.

A community unwilling to gather at the table together to listen to Christ and one another is a community destined for fraction. These conversations are best held at the communion table, because Christ alone hosts and possesses the capability to take us as we are, blessing us as image bearers, breaking us of the rough spots that do not conform to his kingdom vision, and returning us to the world changed into kingdom citizens. Bonhoeffer continues

> A community which cannot bear and cannot survive such a crisis, which insists upon keeping its illusion when it should be shattered, permanently loses in that moment the promise of Christian community . . . He who loves his dream of a community more than the Christian community itself becomes the destroyer of the latter, even though his personal intentions may be ever so honest and earnest and sacrificial.[11]

The table stands open to invitation. Jesus does not force anyone to come to the table, but neither does he turn anyone away. The Gospels reveal a Jesus who welcomes any to his table, but who also challenges guests to become more like him. This offended some guests to the point that they walk away. There is not a single Gospel story of Jesus forcing people to eat dinner with him, nor does he chase down guests who choose to walk away. That is reminiscent of Rublev's icon: the table is always open on the side where the viewer stands. It does not force fellowship. It only invites.

Sadly, the world is full of people who will never come to the table despite the open invitation. Sadder still are the ones who choose to remove themselves from the table. But I fear the most evil of all are those who would seek to drive other diners from the table. Refusing to come to the table with others due to social, ethnic, or theological differences is evidence of ideological colonization.[12] We are not the gatekeepers of God's communion with God's creation. Whenever we begin to believe and act in ways that force our personal perspectives on the table, we are guilty of placing our narratives ahead of God's narrative in Jesus.

Coming to the table requires each person to recognize, as Rublev portrays, the Holy Trinity sitting in a welcoming circle of communion with one another, in constant deference to one another, and as host of the table. This is how we should approach the table: as a community who willingly defers to one another for the sake of fellowship and, most importantly, in deference to the actual hosts. We are not the hosts or guardians of the table; Jesus is the host. In an American culture deeply divided over countless issues and perspectives, the most Christian thing we can do is to yield to one another in love. We may not agree on everything; however, by deferring to one another, especially at the table, we get a little closer to the kingdom of God.

Jesus alone supervises the guest list, and if Isaiah 25 and the New Testament have it right, then the list remains pretty broad and exists with eschatological ramifications. If Andrei Rublev, Dietrich Bonhoeffer, C. S. Lewis, and N. T. Wright are on track, then the discipline of gathering at the present table will require a lot of work from us as we pursue unity and holiness. Each time we break fellowship and communion with others, we do damage to the kingdom of God.

Hope does exist, as Jesus told his disciples in Mark 10:27, "With man this is impossible, but not with God; all things are possible with God." If I seek to be the host, hoping to serve as cosmic bouncer, I am seeking to build my kingdom through force of my ideological colonization and achieving the actual kingdom will be impossible. But if I submit to Christ and humbly gather at the table with others, we might be closer to the kingdom on earth as it is in heaven. Unity and fellowship are not easy, but with Jesus as host all things are possible.

The Practice of Communion Reorients Our Relationships

In one form or another, nearly all Christians participate in communion. Beyond that, of all the spiritual disciplines available to Christians, communion seems to be the one to which we are most faithful. We might gather weekly, monthly, quarterly, or randomly at the table. Sometimes we incorporate the table into significant church and life events like weddings, funerals, or commissioning of clergy, missionaries, and church leaders. We break bread and consume the cup in thousand-year-old cathedrals, brick church houses, nursing home chapels, hospital bedsides, rickety structures, homes, and outdoors. In some traditions only clergy can mediate communion. In other traditions there is no such boundary between clergy and laity, and anyone can usher those gathered into remembrance. Some use wine only, others juice only. Some tear bread from a whole loaf, and others have it served pre-broken. Some share a common cup, and others have small individual cups for each participant. Some drink and others dip. Some are ushered forward to a single table; others bring the elements to the worshipers in their seats.

Variety abounds in our approach to the table. Communion involves the bread and the cup, the priest and the parishioner, the church and the world, the body and the blood, but it is ultimately about presence. When we gather around the table in remembrance and take, bless, break, and give the bread and the cup, we learn to be aware of the presence of Christ. Communion also makes us more aware and connected to the other people gathered around the table. When we gather in communion with fellow believers, and become more aware of Christ's presence at the table, we become more capable of recognizing the presence of Christ in the rest of our lives and the lives of those around us. "If we can be trained into its logic of forgiveness, reconciliation, and renewal on Sunday, we can recognize that same logic of his presence in the world . . . the table . . . trains us to discern Christ's presence in all the other places we eat during the week."[13]

Communion is not just an intellectual exercise; it is a reenactment of Christ's table life. Sharing communion together is a way to participate physically, with words and actions, in our great hope of salvation. Closing the table life gatherings with communion refreshes the community's focus on the gospel. "When we eat and when we drink, we accept and receive and participate in the atoning death of Jesus, the liberating power of the resurrection, and the expectant return of the Lord to establish his kingdom."[14] Each time we gather at the table where Jesus hosts, we enter once again into the dramatic and comprehensive narrative of salvation.

Of all the symbols Jesus could have left his followers, he chose to leave a table. By participating in communion, we participate in the most important form of table fellowship available: "The table ought to be the primary symbol of the Christian community. It represents hospitality, inclusivity, generosity, and grace."[15] Jesus hosts at the communion table, whether in a church, a home, an office building, or a park. The communion table serves as a remembrance of the sacrifice of Christ where his body and blood promise that one day all will be as God intended. But even more than remembering, we engage with the presence of Christ. We learn to see and experience the presence of Christ at the communion table so that we can see it in other places.

By closing the meals with communion, the participants reenact the entire evening one last time. They engage the story of Christ's promise to be present by partaking in his body and his blood. They listen again to the Scriptures. They listen to one another and share in the common narrative when they say, "This is Christ's body broken for you . . . this is the cup of the new covenant." They eat and drink one more time in company with one another and Christ. They respond to the Scriptures and the meal by going forth as brothers and sisters in Christ to tell the story of God.

Here is a way to close in communion at your mealtime fellowship.[16] Prepare in advance the cup and bread. Fill a cup with juice or wine based on your tradition and context. Choose bread that that can be broken or torn easily. Place the elements in a central location where everyone has access, such as the center of the dinner table. Have the group sit around the table where you shared dinner. If you attend an informal dinner that does not include a table, feel free to adapt your space as necessary. Have someone read a short passage of Scripture that reminds those gathered of communion. Some suggested passages include but are not limited to: 1 Corinthians 11:23-26, Isaiah 25:6-8, Matthew 26:26-30, Mark 12:28-32, Mark 14:22-26, or Luke 22:7-22.

After a group member reads the Scripture, someone may wish to offer a few homiletic thoughts on the passage, but this is not required. Have someone offer a prayer of thanksgiving for the bread. Lift the bread for all to see and say, "This is the body of Christ broken for you" while tearing the bread in half. Set one half down, and from the other half tear off a small piece of bread and pass the half loaf around the table, allowing each person present to tear off a piece in turn. While everyone holds their small torn piece of bread, have someone offer a prayer of thanksgiving for the cup. Hold up the cup and say, "This is the cup of the new covenant." Set the cup down and have everyone dip their small piece of bread into the cup and eat their bread. Conclude with brief silence or a short prayer.

As a fun alternative, build the whole night around the communion experience by bookending the gathering with bread and cup. I was recently at a table life meal where the hosts began the evening by welcoming everyone to the table before the meal was set. They did a welcoming prayer and set out the basic outline of the evening. We then participated in the breaking of the bread. They passed the loaf by tearing a piece off and handing it to the person next to us with the blessing, "The body of Christ broken for you." Once everyone had eaten their bread to start the evening, the meal began. We did our Scripture reading and storytelling. When finished, we closed the evening with prayer requests. Once everyone shared, they had small communion glasses for each participant, and we all drank to the blessing, "Cup of the new covenant." We then offered our prayers and thanksgiving to Christ.

Some Additional Thoughts

Communion is an important and common act of worship among Christians. Enjoy the opportunity to lead and be led in new spaces. It does not need to be a stressful or difficult experience. With a little preparation and forethought, sharing communion in a home can be a wonderful experience. It is a good idea to designate the people to read Scripture, pray, and pass the elements in advance so they have time to practice and prepare. While almost all of us have participated in communion as parishioners, many of us have never led in communion. Taking time to think through what will be said and done helps alleviate stress. If you need further guidance, contact your local pastor, deacon, or ministry leaders who regularly lead in communion in the local church.

Within my tradition of the American Baptist Churches USA, we do not make distinctions between clergy and laity in the way some traditions do. We practice a concept of pastors as equal in status to every other member in a church—leaders among equals who can equip the congregation and members for their acts of ministry. We do not require communion to be led by an ordained clergy person. As such we encourage and welcome anybody who wishes to lead and participate in communion to do so as their conscience allows in any context they find themselves.

Some Christian traditions do not permit this same level of freedom in leading communion. If your tradition requires a priest or pastor to lead or oversee a communion experience, ask them about possible freedoms your tradition has that allow for lay-led services. Some traditions may require a clergy blessing of the bread and cup in advance to be distributed by nonordained congregants. Some liturgical traditions will change the name of the event from a Mass or Eucharist to a communion, love feast, or agape meal to distinguish between clergy-led and laity-led experiences. A good example in more liturgical traditions are love feasts. Historically, love feasts include times of singing, personal testimony (storytelling), Scripture reading (dwelling in the Word), guided prayer, and feasting on a common meal. Your tradition may have a book of worship or canon code that provides helpful liturgies for how to participate or lead in-home communion services or love feasts. These resources can be informative, help you prepare for your communion meal, and enrich your understanding of your specific Christian heritage. There is room in most traditions for the taking of communion in a home led by nonordained persons. It just may require a little more research and forethought.

Conclusion

By ending mealtime with communion, you reenact the entire meal. You gather at the table, listen to Scripture, listen to your fellow worshipers, and eat food. It is a time to recognize the presence of the Holy Trinity in your life and the lives of those gathered. The communion table acts as a place of perpetual fellowship and welcome. Taking, blessing, breaking, and giving bread gives life. When we conclude our times of fellowship with communion, we acknowledge our gratitude for the presence of Jesus in our past, present, and future. Communion summarizes the table life experience, but also contains elements of commissioning. We never return to the rhythms of life the same as before we tasted bread and cup and meditated on the Word. Communion changes the heart, mind, and soul. Once the elements are consumed and the good-byes said, we can confidently return to the places where we live, work, and play, looking to encounter Christ more deeply than ever before.

NOTES

1. Eugene H. Peterson, *Christ Plays in Ten Thousand Places: A Conversation in Spiritual Theology* (Grand Rapids, MI: Eerdmans, 2008), 208.

2. Glen Packiam, *Blessed Broken Given: How Your Story Becomes Sacred in the Hands of Jesus* (Colorado Springs, CO: Multnomah, 2019), 27–36.

3. Packiam, *Blessed Broken Given*, 81.

4. Peterson, *Christ Plays in Ten Thousand Places*, 210.

5. David E. Fitch, *Faithful Presence: Seven Disciplines That Shape the church for Mission* (Downers Grove, IL: InterVarsity Press, 2016), 49.

6. Peterson, *Christ Plays in Ten Thousand Places*, 211.

7. Packiam, *Blessed Broken Given*, 135.

8. N. T. Wright, "The Letter to the Ephesians," *Theology in Scotland* 20, no. 2 (2013): 7.

9. C. S. Lewis, *The Screwtape Letters*, Signature Classic (New York: HarperOne, 2015), 81–82.

10. Dietrich Bonhoeffer, *Life Together* (New York: HarperCollins, 2005), 26–27.

11. Bonhoeffer, *Life Together*, 27.

12. "Ideological colonization," a phrase often used by Pope Francis, describes both cultural and spiritual intolerance of differences. Pope Francis used the phrase to point toward a form of oppression of developing societies by affluent ones, especially the West, through imposing an alien worldview or set of values on poorer societies, often by making adoption of those values a condition of humanitarian or development aid. This can be seen religiously when Christians from affluent cultures or denominations seek to force people they see as spiritually weaker or inferior to adopt their theological and social views to be in community and communion.

13. Fitch, *Faithful Presence*, 51.

14. Scot McKnight, *A Fellowship of Differents: Showing the World God's Design for Life Together* (Grand Rapids, MI: Zondervan, 2015), 105.

15. Michael Frost, *Surprise the World: The Five Habits of Highly Missional People* (Colorado Springs, CO: NavPress, 2016), 46.

16. See Appendix D for additional communion liturgy options.

7

New Media and #tablelife

As the lights dim, the anticipation of the audience grows palpable. The confident voice of Gertrude Matshe comes over the speaker system: "If you are looking for me on the stage, you might be looking in the wrong place . . ." and as the lights slowly rise, Matshe walks on stage with the 'TedX TeAro' logo to explain *Ubuntu*, a South African philosophy of community.[1] Matshe wants the audience to not only see her as an individual but as an extension of her community, all with equal voices. Much like our study of the Hebrew word *Shema*, *Ubuntu* holds layers of meaning and implications. Most directly translated into English, *Ubuntu* means "a person is only a person through other people." We need community and run the risk of ruining ourselves if we seek things in total isolation. *Ubuntu* reminds us that life works best when humans live out their connectedness with God and with others. This is what it means to live in the way of Jesus.[2]

As human beings, we thrive in the presence of others. Damaged and flawed community habits are one of the tragic consequences of Genesis 3. The first humans fracture their relationship to God and to one another by eating wrongly. The rest of the primordial story (Gen 1–12) spirals into deeper fractures until human beings build the Tower of Babel. This endeavor splintered and scattered Babylon's community, but beginning with Abraham, the biblical narrative strives toward rescue, rebuilding, and renewal of proper community with God and with others.

Throughout the Bible, God communicates his mission of love and renewal with God's people. We previously looked at how God spoke through winds, fire, and earthquakes with Israel broadly and Elijah in particular. We also read in Scripture how God spoke through angels, prophets, and even a mule. Scripture itself functions as a medium of communication. Most importantly, God demonstrates God's love by becoming human in Jesus. God's care for community prompted God to move beyond all previously used mediums of communication and became one of us. Eugene Peterson's translation of John 1:14 conveys this beautifully: "The Word became flesh and blood, and moved into the neighborhood. We saw the glory with our own eyes, the one-of-a-kind glory, like Father, like Son, Generous inside and out, true from start to finish" (MSG). God, in Jesus Christ, moved into the neighborhood. If that does not communicate God's love for community, I am not sure what else would convince us.

God initiates community and, as image bearers, we are designed to be in community with God and with others. The greatest commandments are to love God and to love others (Mark 12:29-31). How can someone love another with whom they are not in regular relationship? Being in full community includes fully utilizing every means available to us. For the early church, this meant oral stories, shared letters, and traveling ministers retelling the Christian story and sharing how to best live it in their local contexts. Followers of Christ also practiced the multisensory engagement of what we have shared in table life—shared meals, community prayers, reading of Bible and apostolic letters, and regular communion.

Tools of communication shift over time, but we know the church has always utilized every avenue possible to share the gospel. From oral retellings and written letters, mass media, the printing press, radio and television, and now through new media, the church has always found ways to reveal the kingdom of God. Today we can practice meaningful habits of discipleship and experience community through various forms of social media. We can even practice table life.

New Media and The Digital Life

The term "social media" has become an all-inclusive term to describe a host of online sites, technologies, and behaviors. Seminary professor and ordained pastor Angela Williams Gorrell offers some clarity by referring to the ever-expanding universe of social media as "new media."[3] She helpfully breaks down the main platform concepts into four large categories:

1. Social networking sites (e.g., Facebook, Twitter, LinkedIn) are online platforms primarily designed for connecting with other people.
2. User-generated content sites (e.g., YouTube, Flicker, Wikipedia) are online platforms where people can upload content (e.g., videos, photos) they have created, curated, or remixed and share it with other people.
3. Trading and marketing sites (e.g., Amazon, Groupon, Craigslist) are online platforms where people buy, sell, and/or trade material goods.
4. Play and game sites (e.g., Angry Birds, Farmville, The Sims Social) are online platforms for playing internet games with other people.[4]

These spaces have much to offer to help build a community. They create space for us to share ideas, display our personalities, tell stories, and experience validation in ways we may not have otherwise. We go online to extend and share our lived experience with others.

As a result of our constant engagement with new media, our lives exist beyond the physical that surrounds us. We have one life, and it exists in multiple realms as we engage in various spaces—everything touches. This is an amazing opportunity to create and establish community and to communicate the love of Christ. But it can be dangerous if we do not think about how we live our one life. We cannot hope to separate the parts from the whole. We cannot segment our life into neat little pockets of existence where each stand alone. We do not have a home life, a professional life, a fandom life, a family life, a church life, and a social media life unique from one another. We have one life, and this life craves community.

Living a holistic life requires reflection. To truly thrive in a media-saturated culture, it is essential to deeply and intentionally consider the power of new media tools and the content they deliver. "We are the first generation of humans who cannot rely on the earned wisdom of previous generations to help us live with these rapid technological changes."[5] Our church communities ought to come together to discern and articulate a vision of Christ's kingdom for new media engagement, including making decisions about limits for engagement and times of disengagement. New media *does* offer exciting new possibilities for nurturing relationships, expressing identity, improved learning, and discipleship. But new media *will not* fix our contemporary problems or be the sole solution to adaptive challenges we face as individuals and the church.[6] However, a consistent and faithful reflection on how we practice our habits of discipleship across these platforms will allow us to utilize new media to its full potential while avoiding dangerous pitfalls.

CONSUMING RELIGIOUS CONTENT ≠ COMMUNITY

I have a confession to make. Sometimes I don't want to go to church. Some days I feel it would be so much easier to just find my favorite speaker and listen to a well-delivered sermon. Sometimes I just want to go for a walk with my headphones blasting my "church" playlist. Some days I don't even want to do that. I have days when I don't want to do anything at all but watch baseball and hang out at my house. There are days it would just be easier if I didn't have to be present with others and expose myself to their chaos when I don't even know how to deal with my own.

If honest, we could all make this same confession. I truly believe that if you need to skip a Sunday here and there, you might be better for it. For some of us, this might last even longer, requiring whole periods of life spent in intentional withdrawal and reflection. But these are the exceptions. We all know we are better together. We know that if we spend too much time building a faith on our own, we will end up worshiping a god who looks a lot like the person in the mirror. There is a difference between periods of intentional withdrawal or discernment like Jesus (Matthew 4:1-11; Luke 4:1-13) and going off on your own like Jonah. Hebrews 10:23-25 always calls us back to encourage us: "Let us hold unswervingly to the hope we profess, for he who promised is faithful. And let us consider how we may spur one another on toward love and good deeds, not giving up meeting together, as some are in the habit of doing, but encouraging one another—and all the more as you see the Day approaching." I need encouragement from others and to accept the responsibility of encouraging others in the name of Jesus. This requires me to use my days of withdrawal as preparation to be in community with others, even when I may not always feel like it.

Table life helps create rhythms and habits of discipleship that guide us into community with God and others. We have discussed how table life works in the context of small groups meeting together in homes and the local church. However, because our lives are not only lived in physical spaces, and due to various circumstances meeting in person may not always be practical, table life extends into the parts of our lives centered around new media.

Table life, even when practiced through new media platforms, deepens our connection to God, to the church, and to one another. This is important to remember, because a huge difference exists between consuming religious content through new media and exercising Christian community. Watching a YouTube sermon or a RightNow video does not have the same impact as engaging in dialog with someone about the Scripture. We cannot compare reading a blog or downloading a podcast to listening to those we are in relationship nor can we liken downloading the All Recipes app or streaming the latest Guy's Grocery Games to sharing a community meal with multiple generations. Posting a #blessed filtered image in your Instagram story presents an incomplete and sanitized version of our very gritty narratives.

Consuming religious content through the various new media platforms can function as helpful and even encouraging tools if used with purpose. We can learn much from a Bible Project video, be moved by incredible music and art, and even feel inspired by the stories of mission and ministry. However, living fully into the ways of Jesus requires more than consuming curated content. The same principle holds true for any of us who attend a local church, sing the songs, and listen to a sermon, but never engage in the larger mission and ministry of that local church. "Thoughtful streaming and scanning is distinct from thoughtless streaming and scanning . . . this is because theology is embodied, exercised, and practiced. Theology is performative. Theology is not merely a set of beliefs, convictions, or ideas about the nature of God; theology is lived."[7] The theology of loving God and loving others must be lived holistically, online and in person, in the context of a community.

Lived theology requires a willingness to try new things and experiment with God's presence in our lives and our relationships, in person and digitally. The ways we extend table life into our new media encounters will require a willingness to try, fail, and try again. It will require looking at the specifics of online platforms, context, and accessibility in order to stay focused on the bigger concept of community.

Below you will find some examples of actual table life groups who have extended their lives into the platforms of new media.

TABLE AND COMMUNION

A small table life group community that included a few adults and five elementary-aged school children met for several months in the fall and winter. Every two weeks this group would gather in a home and follow a guided mealtime liturgy together. The group acquired this liturgy from another table group they had met online while discerning how to best practice table life in their community. Each table liturgy included a welcome, sharing communion bread, a dinner, Scripture reading and reflection, dialogue questions, prayer of the people, taking the communion cup, and a benediction. Every aspect of the table life group invited both the adults and the children to participate.

I was privileged to join this table group on a couple occasions. Their hospitality was matched only by their passion for looking for Christ's presence in all aspects of life. It was inspiring to watch how adults and children all have roles to play in preparing the meal, setting the table, reading Scripture, liturgy, and prayer. It is an interactive multi-generational table life group in community with one another and their local church.

When the COVID-19 coronavirus quarantine of 2020 went into place, the whole world had to adjust to a variety of "new normal" behaviors. This group's bi-weekly gathering was no exception. They thought and prayed for ways to continue their gatherings while still exercising social distancing. They settled on setting up a live video feed between their homes. In advance of the meal, families emailed PDF copies of that week's liturgy to the rest of the group and assigned leaders for each part. To create a sense of connectedness, each family prepared the same meal and set their tables to simulate the whole group's presence in their homes. Everyone even sat in their usual spots. With the live feed ready and everyone seated, the group began the table liturgy. They ate their meals in their own homes with the live video running, allowing everyone to keep their usual dinner conversations, kids to tell jokes, and adults to catch up with each other. They completed their liturgy as usual with the group signing off once they completed the benediction.

The idea of having meals in your own space while sharing a live video conference is not unique to this table group. The importance of eating with others is well-documented and becomes acutely pronounced during periods of separation, illness, or, as in the case of the coronavirus, quarantine. Ideas such as virtual happy hours and group dinners where people can "eat alone, together"[8] are not new but have gained recent prominence. My family's home sits adjacent to a significant military base. Many of our neighbors have experienced times with deployed loved ones. New media options allow families to stay connected, have conversations, and share virtual meals with their deployed service member over platforms like FaceTime or Google Hangouts.

Eating together, even if it is "eating alone, together" remains important even when extended into the realm of new media. Recipes can be shared in advance via email, text, or shared cooking apps, inviting people to make the same meal. You might even live stream or record your cooking experience to share with your table life group. You can swap recipe alterations via a comment feature on social media. It may not be the same as being in the room with someone, but as an alternative to gathering in person and in the effort of sharing your digital life with another, it is a good place to begin.

Communion practices will also be pushed to their limit in times of isolation for the same reasons as dinner. The bread and the cup are physical things that cannot be shared the same way through an HD camera, yet taking the time to slow down our pace and participate in the habit of communion, even when we cannot meet in person, is a worthy practice.

Taking communion with others helps us prioritize table life amid a culture that endorses hectic schedules with hurried meals between activities or binge-watching sessions. By slowing down and sharing communion, even if through a video conference, reminds us that we are not like the machines that facilitate digital community. We need sustenance. We are dependent upon God and upon others. We pray it each time we say the Lord's Prayer—"Your kingdom come, Your will be done . . . give us this day our daily bread."

Ultimately, we are dependent upon things outside of ourselves. Food helps remind us of this. Every morsel of food we consume appears on our plate out of our dependence upon our neighbors; someone somewhere had to plant, tend, harvest, butcher, inspect, transport, stock, and serve the food we eat.[9] Local communion encourages us to reflect on our dependence upon God and others, even as we view our table life companions across a screen.

Much like table life around a common table, communion through new media platforms does not need to be overly complicated. To borrow the expression above, taking "communion alone, together" might require adaptations, but the practice itself should not be brushed aside. Sometimes a table life group needs to gather online. Participants will need to provide their own elements for communion. Whatever bread and juice we bring to the practice is enough. Utilizing the communion liturgies provided in the appendix will help guide participants through communion. The significant difference is the passing of bread and cup. If multiple people share a single screen, they can serve one another. Otherwise, everyone can feel free to partake of their own bread and cup at their locations.

Jesus' presence in the bread and the cup endures as a holy mystery. Nearly every Christian theological perspective on communion asserts Christ's presence. Not every perspective agrees on how, but we do all agree that somewhere between bread and cup, and the Holy Spirit and the people of God, something happens. Video conferencing allows us to be present to one another—in unity, real bodies, real bread, and the real presence of the Triune God.[10] In eating alone, we can eat together in Christ.

DWELLING IN THE WORD

As the grid of faces smiled out of the screen, Christ's presence clearly appeared. After a snowstorm, the table life group decided not to chance the roads, although they still wanted to meet. The group leader created a live video conference call for everyone to use to check in and engage in prayer with the intent to continue their regular table life group gathering in a few weeks. The group remembers this particular video conference call as one of their best dwelling in the Word experiences. Participants later recalled the meaningfulness of the experience, specifically that everyone shared more freely, with more time to think about their reflections, and felt less self-conscious through the filter of computer screen.

Video conferencing and group audio calls are more accessible than ever. Platforms like Zoom, Skype, GoToMeeting, and Google Hangouts provide spaces for people to interact with one another in powerful ways. For disciplines like dwelling in the Word, prayer, and storytelling, these platforms create space for people to communicate at a deeper level than phone or written words alone. Our best communication happens when we both hear and see the other person. We have all misread the tone of an email or comment on a social media feed. The non-verbal clues of body posture, facial expressions, and matching verbal tones help add depth to conversations. With these clues, we get the full range of meaning in a comment.

Dwelling in the Word, especially, naturally translates to video conferencing platforms. Dwelling also creatively extends into other new media platforms as well. For example, a group may choose to dwell on the Emmaus Road passage from Luke 24. Everyone shares the word or phrase most meaningful to them and how it connects to other observations in the group. To extend that conversation into the new media, the group could use a private Facebook group or Messenger feature to make further observations through the next two weeks on the passage. They might share their daily experiences, other revelations about the passage, or how the passage helped them recognize Jesus' accompaniment on the road with them in everyday tasks. A group might challenge each person to research and post an image or icon on their Instagram that reflects the passage. People in the group can also share comments about the image's connection to the biblical text. All this can be done in real-time through new media so the conversation is constant and immediately reflective, rather than having to wait for the next time the group gathers in person.

An image that connects the Emmaus Road journey for me is Vincent van Gogh's *The Potato Eaters*. Vincent van Gogh, a Dutch post-impressionist artist of the late nineteenth century, is best known for his struggles with mental health, severing his own ear, and his amazing works of art such as *The Starry Night, The Sower,* and his various self-portraits. As a young man, van Gogh's zeal for Christ led him to first try to become a minister, then a missionary in a coal mining town in southern Belgium, before returning home to pursue art. Through these experiences, he struggled with his love of God, the chaos of the world, and, at least in his experience, the church's lack of compassionate mercy towards impoverished people like those he met in Belgium. Van Gogh eventually developed a colorful artistic style, portraying images of landscapes, still-life's, and portraits. His favorite color to represent the presence of God in his paintings was yellow—a color noticeably absent from the windows of the churches in *The Starry Night* and *Starry Night Over the Rhone,* yet wildly visible in his landscapes like *The Sower.*

Early on in his artistic pursuits he painted a much grittier portrait called *The Potato Eaters* that displays a humble family sharing a simple dinner around a table under a single light. Even in this early work, you can begin to see his love of yellow to display the presence of the divine. The single gas flame above the table gives the work its light source, casting a faint glow over the meal and the faces of the family. The family members' eyelines eerily match those of Rublev's angels, deferring to one another. They are in mutual humility and community with one another.

The work also resembles communion in the pouring of the coffee: a cup received in gratitude, and the potatoes in a single common dish with no other plates on the table. You can almost hear the voice of Christ comforting the family from the lamp and the small portrait of the crucifixion on the wall in the background: "This is my body, this is my blood."

This painting of a humble family gathered for a meal also shares the power of the Luke 24 Emmaus Journey story: "When he [Jesus] was at the table with them, he took bread, gave thanks, broke it and began to give it to them. Then their eyes were opened and they recognized him . . ." (Luke 24:30-31a). As this family gathers at the table, and shares their coffee and potatoes, the presence of Christ emerges. This is the type of image one might share on social media to continue the conversation of table life and add a new element to a dwelling in the Word experience.

LISTENING AND STORYTELLING

New media platforms, such as YouTube, Instagram, Facebook, TikTok, Snapchat, and Twitter, allow people to post original content and share existing content with others in your networks. Every platform has its limitations. TikTok and Instagram, for example, limit videos to less than 60 seconds. YouTube will not allow songs with copyright privileges as the video audio unless posted by the creator. Instagram will not permit a user to embed a link into your story until you have a verified account with over 10,000 followers. Finally, every site uses its own proprietary algorithms to determine when and where your content appears in other people's feeds, which requires a great deal of hard work if you want your content seen by certain people. Being aware of the strength and weakness of each platform allows you to capitalize on the best uses of new media to extend community in different ways.

A word of caution. There are inherent risks to publicly sharing, consuming, and interacting with any new media platform. The internet is forever. Every video, every post, every comment is archived and searchable, forever. The ever-changing privacy settings for posting and sharing mean nothing is guaranteed indefinitely. A reasonable amount of precautions must be exercised when using these types of new media for table life purposes. Each platform also hosts a variety of content that may be controversial or downright offensive. Use wise discretion when exploring content on any new media platform.

After a series of troubling local and national news events a pastor recently observed a high level of pain and anxiety sharing on social media by those in his network. He created a conversation asking people to share their grief, posting on Facebook, "The grief coming through social media right now is immeasurable. We have no place to put it. What grief would you put here, just to give it a place outside of your own heart?" The responses were raw, honest, and public. With great pastoral care and skill, this pastor responded to every comment with love and compassion. This single Facebook post had dozens of responses creating an opportunity for people to share their stories of lament amid heartache. This new media platform provided space for this pastor and those who could view his posts to listen to the story and experience of others in their community context to reflect on what God is doing during a time of difficulty. The post served as an extension of everyday life and allowed the pastor to move some of the conversations offline to begin to walk with the commenters further down the Emmaus Road to see Christ at the table.

Video conference platforms such as Zoom, Skype, or FaceTime might hold a bit more confidentiality and intimacy than a public Facebook feed and operate more like a private phone call, especially when such interactions require a password to access. Recording features exist, but I encourage users to disable those features for the purpose of table life. Trust when sharing and listening to others' personal narratives remains vital. It also emphasizes the need to be fully present in the moment. Many of these platforms also have breakout room features where smaller subgroups can gather for conversation. This would be a fun way for a whole church community to gather together and share updates, prayer requests, and announcements before breaking into smaller table life groups.

When practicing the spiritual disciplines of storytelling and listening through an online platform, there are a few things to consider. Let's begin with storytelling. As discussed previously, the ability to share your story in under twenty minutes is important. However, the online platform gives the storyteller some creative abilities that might not be readily possible without some awkwardness in an in-person setting. The storyteller in a video conference can share their screen, allowing the person to show pictures, share videos, or display a Prezi or PowerPoint Presentation. Perhaps the most creative among us can utilize these platforms to create videos or encourage people to watch a video, check out a social media feed, or visit a website in advance to supplement the story.

The important thing to remember when sharing your story through new media is to minimize distractions. Keep avoidable background noise away from the microphone and unnecessary movement off camera. Use good front-facing lighting to ensure listeners can see your face and take in those all-important non-verbal communication cues. If you plan on sharing content that requires screen sharing or displaying something in your physical space, practice those switches in advance to avoid clumsy transitions or unintended silence.

Be creative and have fun with your storytelling, but double check to make sure everything is in order before going live.

Storytelling requires listeners. When listening to another person's story, give yourself to the moment just as you would around a dinner table with others. Listening online might require more focus than listening to someone in-person. Do not multi-task during the listening portion of table life. Eliminate as many distractions as possible. The space where you listen should not be a place of disruption for you. Avoid practicing listening skills while driving a car, in a busy shopping center, or on a walk, for example. These are great places for audio books and podcasts, but not for community listening. Close all other applications on your computer or smart device to avoid notifications interrupting the storyteller on your screen. This is not the time to respond to email, comment on social media posts, or have the big game on in the background. Do your best to make digital eye contact by looking at the person speaking (and occasionally looking directly at the camera) and respond with your own non-verbal clues like nodding your head to let the storyteller know you are engaged. Being a good listener is how we give the grace-filled gift of reciprocity for the storyteller.

Conclusion

Today, the use of smart devices and social media platforms comes from a desire to connect. Microsoft researchers have noted that "most teens are not compelled by gadgetry as such—they are compelled by friendship. The gadgets are interesting to them primarily as a means to a social end."[11] New media and devices are not the end in and of themselves, but rather vehicles that provide the means for building and experiencing community.

I graduated high school in 2000 and did not have a cell phone until I was a sophomore in college or a social media account until I was in graduate school. I am probably part of the final generation to glorify turning 16 and getting a driver's license. In my hometown, there was a strip of road between the Riverside Park at one end and the Citgo gas station a half-mile away at the other. Between these two landmarks, local students would "cruise the strip" on weekends. Cars and trucks filled the shoulder of the road, a car wash, an open field (now a shopping plaza), and the parking area of the Riverside Park. It was customary to pick a spot to park and get out of your vehicle to chat and visit with others. Just past the cruising strip were a series of fast-food chain restaurants. It was not uncommon to see combo-deals consumed from the bed of a pickup or atop the hood of a car. When you were ready to hang out with other students, or pilfer someone else's fries, you and your core group of friends would fill a vehicle to capacity and look for a new pocket of people to visit. For us the technology of the vehicle allowed us to be in community with others. Most of us were not car-loving gearheads; we were community people, and the car made spending time with others possible. Every generation and context have that thing that brings them together.

This is what new media technology does for us now, only on a much larger scale. Social media and smart devices create community like the car did for me in my teens. It provides the ability to connect and build community. But much like learning to safely drive a car, we must know what to do before we simply dive in and start using these platforms and devices with no discernment. We must choose wisely which platforms extend table life by furthering community and avoid those which simply call us toward ever deeper levels of consumerism and isolation.

NOTES

1. Gertrude Matshe, "Ubuntu - a person is a person through other persons," YouTube video, 18:40, posted by "Tedx Talks," August 3, 2013, https://www.youtube.com/watch?v=BzIyOtusDxE.

2. Scot McKnight, *One.Life: Jesus Calls, We Follow* (Grand Rapids, MI: Zondervan, 2010), 32–34.

3. Angela Williams Gorrell, *Always On: Practicing Faith in a New Media Landscape* (Grand Rapids, MI: Baker Academic, 2019), 2.

4. Gorrell, *Always On*, 2–3. Gorrell concedes: "However, there are many sites that mix platforms. For example, Facebook connects people, allows people to upload created content and invite others to play games, and has created ways for people to buy, sell, and trade items through its site."

5. David Kinnaman and Mark Matlock, *Faith for Exiles: 5 Ways to Help a New Generation Follow Jesus and Thrive in Digital Babylon* (Grand Rapids, MI: Baker Academics, 2019), 25.

6. Gorrell, *Always On*, 25–33.

7. Gorrell, *Always On*, 42–43.

8. Emily Heil, "Eating Alone, Together: Virtual Dinner Parties Are Helping People Fight Isolation." Washington Post, March 21, 2020, sec. 1. https://www.washingtonpost.com/news/voraciously/wp/2020/03/21/eating-alone-together-virtual-dinner-parties-are-helping-people-fight-isolation/.

9. Justin Whitmel Early, *the common Rule: Habits of Purpose for an Age of Distraction* (Downers Grove, IL: InterVarsity Press, 2019), 49–51.

10. Ridgeway, Chris. "Online Communion Can Still Be Sacramental." ChristianityToday.com. Accessed April 13, 2020. https://www.christianitytoday.com/ct/2020/march-web-only/online-communion-can-still-be-sacramental.html.

11. Dana Boyd, *It's Complicated: The Social Lives of Networked Teens* (New Haven: Yale University Press, 2014), 18.

8

Emmaus Journey to the Table

The story of the travelers to Emmaus in Luke 24:13-35 has captured the imagination of Christ followers since that first Easter morning when Cleopas and his companion hit the road to mourn the loss of Jesus. There is something relatable about the walkers as they share their grief with one another and with an unrecognized Jesus. They seem to have a blocked vision of the Messiah and how his kingdom works. As Jesus opens the Scripture to them, their hearts stir. As Jesus breaks bread with them, their eyes recognize Jesus in their midst.

Each one of us can relate to different elements of the journey. Each of us has had moments of such blinding sorrow we cannot see Jesus standing right next to us. We too have consequential encounters that stir something inside us like a burning fire. We have had moments of clarity, those "aha" moments when the mysteries of the world seem to slide into place like a complicated jigsaw puzzle, however brief.

The walk from Jerusalem to Emmaus, and the hurried dash back to Jerusalem, help to pull all the elements of a table life into a single narrative. If stories matter and give us hope, then the one about two people who walked from a room filled with sorrow in Jerusalem to a dinner table hosted by Jesus in Emmaus should be one that shapes our hearts, minds, and souls.

Listening

Luke 24:13 begins with "Now that same day." Any story that begins with a preface like that requires us to look a little further back to understand how we got to this moment. In this case, we do not need to go further back than the beginning of Luke 24 to gain our bearings. Mary Magdalene, Joanna, Mary the mother of James, and a group of other, unnamed women wake up early in the morning and make their way toward a garden tomb to anoint the dead body of Jesus. When they arrive on the scene, they immediately know something is wrong, or at least they may find something unexpected. The tombstone has been moved, and the cave is empty.

To fully embrace the chaos and wonderful joy of this first Easter morning, we must remember that no one expected Jesus to rise from the dead. No one! The beginning of the resurrection story begins with a group of women traveling to a garden tomb with spices, oils, and linens in hand, expecting to anoint a dead body. Instead they find the tomb empty and the first chapter to a new narrative.

To add to the unfamiliar, two men in blinding white clothing appear and begin to shed some light on the situation: "Why do you look for the living among the dead? He is not here; he has risen!" (vv. 5-6). The men in white call upon the women to remember what Jesus told them before his death: "Remember how he told you, while he was still with you in Galilee: 'The Son of Man must be delivered over to the hands of sinners, be crucified and on the third day be raised again.' Then they remembered his words" (vv. 6-8). I love that word *remember*. It means to recollect or bring into your mind an awareness of something from the past. If these faithful women are called to remember the words of Jesus, then they were present when Jesus gave these teachings in first place. They, as fellow disciples, are called to recollect their previous listening experiences with Jesus, to bring the stories and promises of Jesus to the front of their hearts and minds.

The women leave the tomb and become the first evangelists. They return to the place where eleven apostles and a group of other disciples are gathered. They tell the story of their morning adventure to the tomb, emphasizing that the tomb was empty and the challenge to remember what Jesus had said while they were all in Galilee together. Peter races to the tomb for corroboration and is left pondering what he has seen and heard.

"Now that same day" (v. 13) two spiritually and emotionally confused travelers walk toward a town called Emmaus. The fact there were two travelers includes a couple of impactful layers for the reader. In Jewish tradition, and the first-century world when these travelers lived, two people were required to confirm the testimony of events. It sets up the listener to hear news that will be important enough to require confirmation. It is interesting that Deuteronomy 19:15 requires two witnesses to convict a person of any crime. Further, Deuteronomy 17:6 specifically requires two or more witnesses to convict someone of a capital offense like homicide. Now it will take two people to bear witness to the reality of resurrection.

Second, Luke uses two people for the sake of ministry and mission multiple times in these writings. The two witnesses of Anna and Simeon prophesy that the infant Jesus is the Messiah. Jesus summons some of his disciples in pairs like when he calls on the brothers of Simon and Andrew, James and John. The seventy disciples are sent out in pairs (Luke 10) to bear witness to the coming of the Messiah. Jesus sends two disciples into Bethphage to commandeer a donkey for his triumphal entry into Jerusalem. A vision of two angels appears before the women at the tomb to proclaim Jesus has risen. This and many other times New Testament authors use pairs to strengthen their writings. Pairs express an important concept in ministry.

The couple on the road to Emmaus are said to be disciples. They may have also been a husband and wife, Cleopas and Mary. John 19:25 describes them this way, although the spelling of their names changes, and includes Mary sitting at the foot of the cross and witnessing Jesus' crucifixion. Though we cannot be sure of this, I like to imagine them as a married couple walking from Jerusalem back home to Emmaus discussing the events of the past few days. Cleopas talks about the teachings of Jesus, how they cheered him into Jerusalem the week prior with shouts of "Hosanna," and how he believed Jesus was a great prophet. Mary reflects on the miracles, the meals, and the horror she witnessed three days prior. Their discussions might include their reservations about the stories of the women visiting the tomb. They are hesitant to believe in something so unprecedented as resurrection, because it hurt too much to give in to such hope in case it turned out to be untrue. The disciples safely believe that the life to which they devoted themselves is now over. Their hope died three days prior.

While in deep discussion, the resurrected Jesus approaches them and asks what they are talking about so intensely. The question stops them in their tracks. They look down at their feet. Then Cleopas and his traveling companion retell the basic events of the life of Jesus. They spell out their previous hopes and belief in Jesus as a powerful prophet who would redeem Israel, just as Zechariah and the prophets promised. They share about his death and the dreams lost in his death. They also tell of their confusion about reports of the empty tomb. They openly confess their struggle to believe in the resurrection.

Jesus lets them tell their story until they finish. He then begins his encounter with these wounded disciples by listening. We must learn to become better listeners of people on the road to Emmaus. As Christians, we desperately want people to know about our hope in the resurrected Jesus. We feel eager to share that hope with others and often put the cart before the proverbial horse. We jump into people's lives, oftentimes unannounced, and honestly unwelcomed, and we start telling them about sin and grace, redemption and resurrection, the cross and the church, and the love of Jesus. All those things are good and true. The world has been redeemed and is filled with the grace of Christ. The church is vital to our interactions with the kingdom of God and God's created world. Of course, Jesus loves people. But he demonstrates that love by listening.

Many people in our world walk on their own Emmaus Road. Perhaps they walk in disappointment. Maybe they walk away from hope. Or they may even walk away from the church just as these two walked away from Jerusalem and their fellow disciples. When Jesus comes upon such people on the road of life, he does not begin with a resurrection sermon. He does not open with "ta-da . . . look at me, I'm totally alive!" He knows people don't always have the ability to hear or see. Most have a hard time believing it even when they do. These two disciples had spent time with Jesus before the crucifixion and resurrection, and they don't even recognize Jesus. How can we expect those who may have even less exposure to Jesus to recognize and know his presence any better? We see Jesus invite the travelers into a conversation by asking, "What are you two talking about?" The openness and vulnerability of the question creates space for those on the road to share themselves. They start talking, and Jesus listens. They talk some more, and Jesus listens some more. When they finally finish, only then does Jesus begin to reshape their imaginations.

We need to learn to listen better. We must create intentional space in our hearts and at our tables for others to share their stories. We must stop interrupting people, attempting to finish their thoughts. We must pay attention and listen to their pain, sorrow, disappointment, and lost hope. When we listen well, we will also hear what motivates and shapes the hearts and minds of the speakers.

This will take time. And it will drive you crazy, especially when you feel like you have the answer sitting there on the tip of your tongue. But we must wait and listen, just as Jesus does with these two travelers. Listening validates them as people and image bearers of God, proves you care about them, and allows you to embody the hope you have in Jesus.

Listening connects us to the biblical narrative, to Christ, and to our community. To be a table life people, we must listen as Jesus listens. If we hope Jesus listens to us, then we should listen to others. Listening the way Jesus listens opens the door for community to develop.

Dwelling in the Word

Jesus listens and reveals himself through the Scriptures: "How foolish you are, and how slow to believe all that the prophets have spoken! Did not the Messiah have to suffer these things and then enter his glory?" Then Jesus walks them through the Scriptures again, explaining how the entirety of Scripture points toward him (Luke 24:25-27).

Jesus offers the world's greatest Bible study, and Luke does not write it down. Even so, Jesus does what the New Testament writers do later: he reveals how the entire canon of Scripture reveals God's redemption story through Jesus. New Testament authors do not spend much energy attempting to proof text the person and purpose of Jesus. To be sure, there are plenty of specific verses from the books of Moses, the Psalms, the prophets, and the writings that describe the mission and ministry of Jesus in advance. But mostly the New Testament authors show how the sum whole of Scripture points to Jesus and how Jesus fulfills not just a few favorite or key verses, but the entire narrative of God's engagement with creation. They speak of the kingdom of God.

Cleopas made this mistake, and possibly caused his grief. Cleopas, like many others, hoped Jesus would be the one to redeem Israel—a hope that the Jewish narrative moved forward toward an eschatological end where all nations would gather at the throne of God. This hope had started, stuttered, endured setbacks and even disasters along the way, but nonetheless it was a narrative with forward momentum. That hope was rooted in a few key verses from places like Isaiah, Zechariah, and the Psalms. There were many such messianic hopes: hope in a military messiah who would crush Roman oppressors and establish a new rule; hope for a spiritual leader who would redeem the holy remnant most faithful to Scripture and the Hebrew people; hope for a son of David to come and reestablish a political dynasty. Yet the entirety of Scriptures points toward a more nuanced, unique vision of all these hopes—the story Jesus reveals to the travelers on the road and what the New Testament authors reveal to us today. Jesus lies within the key verses and phrases familiar to us, including every word and letter in between them. We frequently miss this part.

The whole narrative of Scripture centers on God's mission to redeem and restore humanity as God originally intended and establish God's kingdom on earth as it is in heaven. Scripture also focuses on Israel's need for both a ruling king of the universe and a suffering servant to die on behalf of all people, not just a chosen people. This narrative tells his redemptive resurrection and the new life brought to all of creation. Jesus fulfills all those promises. Jesus has now entered his glory through the power of resurrection, and the kingdom of God on earth begins to take place. For as Jesus reminds us, to take a proof-text approach misses the point: "How foolish you are and how slow to believe all that the prophets have spoken!" (v. 25). Jesus opens the entire canon of Scripture to the travelers to reveal the identity of the Messiah: "And beginning with Moses and all the Prophets, he explained to them what was said in all the Scriptures concerning himself" (v. 27). Every letter and word and every space in between every letter and word reveals the story of Jesus.

We must be able to navigate Scripture like Jesus and the New Testament authors. We must become better students of the narrative of Scripture from Genesis 1 to Revelation 22, or as my high-school Sunday school teacher would say, "From the table of contents to the maps." If the risen Christ on the first Easter day made himself known through the entire narrative of Scripture, then we should not suppose we can make him known any other way. No amount of human wisdom, philosophy, revelation, or self-righteous arguments can tell you the meaning of the resurrection. Nobody in Luke 24 has a clue until Jesus explains it from the Bible . . . only then do their hearts burn and eyes open.

New Testament writers could write about Jesus as the fullness of Scripture by dwelling within that story every day. Their familiarity with the story allowed them to share that with others. A table life requires us to dive deeply into the biblical narrative. It also requires that we read the narrative in a community. Jesus shared the narrative of Scripture with just two disciples here, but later in Luke 24 he will reveal it to the eleven apostles and other disciples. The earliest disciples spent time reading Scripture daily as a group. If we want to experience the kind of community power they did, we will read the Scriptures with others.

Table Life and Communion

The three travelers eventually arrive at a home in Emmaus. Cleopas and his companion are not quite ready to be done. As they enter their home, they insist Jesus stays with them for dinner. Hospitality is a key element to the first-century culture, and even in their weary, confused state they refuse to allow this traveler to carry on alone without a full stomach and some rest.

Can you imagine the scene? Jesus, Cleopas, and possibly his wife, Mary, have just walked a good distance on foot. They arrive at the house and must make supper. They gather wood for a fire for light and cooking, ingredients from the cupboards, pull down the mixing bowls and set the pots and pans on the wood-fire stove. They make quick bread on a clay pan over coals, pour some olive oil over some vegetables, and pull the salted fish from the clay pot in the corner. They fill cups with wine and water, light a few candles and oil lamps, and perhaps eat some small amount of lamb left over from the Passover feast in Jerusalem. They say their mealtime prayers.

Perhaps Jesus shares in the preparations. Like any guest attending a dinner party, he helps the hosts. He stirs the oil into the vegetables, tends the fire, and helps set the table, all while discussing the loveliness of their home and favorite family recipes.

Once the food is prepared and the table set, the three of them sit on threadbare cushions around the low table. Gathered around this basic but lovingly prepared meal, Jesus takes the opportunity to assume the role of host. Jesus takes the warm bread into his nail-pierced hands and lifts it into view for everyone in the room to see and blesses the bread. Cleopas and his companion look up into the eyes of Jesus and start to see him for the first time in hours. His words . . . the cadence . . . the rhythm . . . the focus is all so familiar. They know these words of blessing deep in their souls. As Jesus breaks the bread, the tears begin to well up in their eyes. Their hearts explode with joy at the possibility of resurrection. Jesus holds out the bread for Cleopas and Mary to take, the scales fall from their eyes, and they no longer see a stranger. They see the resurrected Jesus. They see his smile and recognize the loving intensity of his eyes. They notice the nail marks in the hands and the familiar way he leans forward to pass the bread. They remember his words on the road and realize he was with them the whole time. Jesus is indeed alive and sitting in their presence holding bread as host of the table.

Just like that, he leaves to present himself to others and turn their sorrow into joy and hope.

Jesus spends most of his time in Luke and the other Gospels either arriving at a meal, at a meal itself, or just leaving a meal. Jesus takes, blesses, breaks, and gives bread hundreds of times with his disciples. Jesus takes, blesses, breaks, and gives, in that order, at the Passover dinner four days earlier. It is no wonder that when he performs this mundane and common act, the disciples of Cleopas and his fellow traveler recognize Jesus. Jesus carried out these acts more than any other.

Jesus wants us to see him eating in order to recognize the renewal and fulfillment of the resurrection. Jesus' resurrection promises the future as a physical future in a newly created heaven and earth. Our salvation story does not center on removal from this world, but rather active engagement with it. It's a future centered around a banquet meal with hot bread, cheesy potatoes, and the best cuts of Nebraska beef. Isaiah 25:6-8 reminds us, "On this mountain the LORD Almighty will prepare a feast of rich food for all peoples, a banquet of aged wine—the best of meats and the finest of wines. On this mountain he will destroy the shroud that enfolds all peoples, the sheet that covers all nations; he will swallow up death forever." At this banquet of the resurrected, all people will enjoy a meal with the resurrected Messiah. This is the image of heaven! The future heaven and earth will be a physical place where people eat, laugh, and enjoy the eternal presence of the Trinity.

The resurrected Jesus making himself known through taking, blessing, breaking, and giving bread makes perfect sense. The disciples from Emmaus recognize Jesus at the table because they connect the narrative told by Jesus on the road with the breaking of the bread at the table. Their eyes open through sharing their story, listening to Jesus, dwelling on the Scriptures, and breaking bread.

A table life is shaped by bread and cup and gathers us around the table to eat with others. It also gathers us around the table to remember with others. Oftentimes, recognizing Jesus around the table causes us to miss Jesus in other places. Living a table life conditions us to see Jesus at the table to then allow us to see Jesus on the road.

Storytelling

Overwhelmed with joy, Cleopas and Mary immediately get up and hastily return to Jerusalem to report their experiences. Upon their arrival, Cleopas and Mary learn that Jesus also appeared to Peter sometime that same day. This reveals once again that Jesus is always one step ahead of us.

Storytelling invites us to recall encounters of our life with others. The women who left home before dawn to place spices in a tomb returned to their community with a new story to tell. They shared their experiences with the group no matter how improbable their testimony seemed. When Cleopas and his companion return to the disciples in Jerusalem, they listen to the story of Jesus appearing to Simon. When it is their turn, Cleopas and Mary tell their story: meeting Jesus on the road and not recognizing him; Jesus opening the Scriptures, deeply moving them; and finally recognizing Jesus as he took, blessed, broke, and gave the bread at dinner.

Storytelling is the stuff of life. We share our experiences from our first-person perspective. It does not need to be elaborate or embellished. Storytelling mostly relies on sharing your heart with others. Not every story is a Simon Peter story filled with moments of great faithfulness and deep denial, though most of us can relate to aspects of his journey. Some of us can tell stories of radical conversion like the apostle Paul. Others of us have stories more like that of Cleopas and have walked away from our communities of faith only to return in joy after seeing Jesus in a whole new way.

We all have a story to tell. Our stories make us unique. No two are the same even if some experiences and elements overlap. Learning to craft your story is part of the journey. Your story is the story of Christ's presence in your life, especially the moments you don't recognize him until much later like the travelers on the Emmaus Road. Our calling as followers of Jesus is to learn to become more aware of the presence of Christ in our lives and to respond to them. We can be honest and admit there are times when he feels distant. But we are always just one broken piece of bread away from seeing his face at our tables and realizing he has been there all along.

Conclusion

Eating meals, listening, storytelling, Scripture, and communion all exist as aspects of our lives. They are primal and basic to every experience and encounter as followers of Christ. We need food to survive. We require the company of others. We need to share our lives and our tables with others to thrive. Jesus dwells in the midst of it all. He is in every shopping line, every soccer practice, every social media post, every spreadsheet, every first date, every funeral, and every hospital room. Jesus is present in the mundane, ordinary stuff of life. He is in constant communion with his creation and every creative interaction in which we participate.

The journey to Emmaus tells a story of two people encountering the living Christ in the most common of places: on a walking path and at a dining room table. He is in the bread and the cup. The Emmaus Road story offers a story of faith, perhaps even the best that Luke writes. It powerfully conveys all our experiences in a condensed, distilled, memorable, and relatable story. Each of us has found ourselves on the road of doubt and confusion. Coming to the table is the beginning of loving acceptance and clarity.

9
Final Thoughts

Table life is a holistic approach to faith and life. Actively engaging in the habits of discipleship and table fellowship—listening, storytelling, reading Scripture as narrative, and communion—help us stay focused on the kingdom of God in our communities. We are hard-wired to flourish within the context of community. We need to be loved and reciprocate love. Table life creates space for us to recognize Christ at our tables and in our communities. By gathering regularly with a community of people to eat and share the spaces where life and faith intersect, we learn to submit to something bigger than ourselves and our personal preferences.

Table life is both taught and caught. Learning to participate faithfully in the five habits of discipleship invites us to see God's presence in our life and the lives of those in our community. The five habits of table life function as spiritual practices, and we must repeat them over long periods of time to where they become engrained into our hearts, minds, and souls. In this way they can be taught. We can be taught how to host a meal, dwell in the Word, guide others in communion, listen better, and craft a story in person and through new media platforms. There are basic skills we can acquire that make us better at these activities. We can also be taught how to look for the presence of Christ in these practices and in our contexts.

Much like the half-truths that shape our various narratives, deeper truths are caught when we practice a table life. When we allow the Scriptures to soak into our very being, we start to notice how the other narratives that surround us are woefully incomplete. When we practice listening to God and others, we begin to realize the rich tapestry of life all around us. As we become more aware of our own story and gain confidence in communicating it to others, we begin to see the rhythms of Christ's presence on the road with us. When we come to the table where Father, Son, and Holy Spirit are in communion with one another as well as break bread and drink the cup with others, we are more equipped to see Christ in the ordinary.

When practiced in our homes, neighborhoods, churches, and via new media platforms, our children, neighbors, and co-workers catch these habits of discipleship. They notice the language we use to describe the world in which we live. They catch on to the hope we have in community. It creates space for them to ask questions about how faith and life intersect for us. Our children grow up knowing they are always welcome at the table, catching the practices and habits for themselves until practicing these habits is a natural way of existing. Practicing such habits regularly provides new lenses for us to look at the world.

Communities that look for ways to connect must spend time together. Jesus strengthened his community of disciples by regularly eating with them and inviting the neighbors from every town they visited. Jesus called all who gather at his table brothers and sisters. If we wish to see our fellow congregants as brothers and sisters, we must spend time with them over dinner, listening to their stories and the story of Scripture. We will see Christ in our midst as we take, bless, break, and give to one another just as Christ does for us.

A friend of mine pastors a city church in the heart of the South Willamette Valley in Oregon. The church has a long history as a meaningful presence in its community. The current building was constructed in 1958, with their sanctuary added ten years later. The sanctuary has a flexible design. Their pews are mobile and can be moved for special occasions. During Lent 2019, my friend moved the communion table from the stage and placed it in the middle of the seating area. He then had to move all the pews so that all seating faced the table in the middle. This had the added benefit of every congregant facing at least the other half of the congregation, while looking through the communion table.

For several weeks the congregation focused on the communion table. Every sermon, every announcement given, every greeting, every song played, and every reading was done while looking at the table. The table became the lens through which they viewed their worship experience. The communion table welcomed each parishioner into the work of Christ in the past and his continued presence in their community contexts.

I think this is a great way to think about table life. As they gathered for worship, sitting around the communion table, each congregant gazed into the face of another community member. It is probably an intensely uncomfortable feeling in a place where people are used to facing the same direction, like looking at a stage. When they sat in the circle, communion table sitting in the middle of the room slightly obscures each face. They must look through the communion table to truly see their brothers and sisters in Christ.

This is what a table life does. It creates space for us to see the world through the lens of Christ's active workings in our lives and communities. The table creates space for us to listen. The table creates space for us to be seen and loved and valued. The table creates space for us to meditate on the narrative of Scripture and to see that Christ is with us everywhere we go.

Table life intentionally fosters habits of discipleship that help us recognize the presence of Christ in a community and focuses on education and action. The table is the place where we put the teachings of Jesus into practice and becomes the place where everything touches: the church and the neighborhood, faith and life, confession and forgiveness, listening and storytelling, dwelling and doing, communion and community.

Appendix A

Dwelling in the Word[1]

Dwelling in the Word invites us to listen for God in our community. We are shaped by the narrative of Scripture. It is the foundation for all we believe and practice. It is only natural that the first place we search for God's voice around the table would be to dwell in the written Word and ask how God calls us to respond to Scripture. Christians believe God speaks to us as individuals through Scripture, and therefore we must listen to one another to hear what God says to our fellow Christians.

As part of your meal experience, dwelling in the Word will shape and guide your community. It is a way to focus your attention on how God asks each of us individually to respond. As you journey through a meal, use the dwelling in the Word portion to help ask, "Where might the Spirit be calling us to respond to God in our context?"

Dwelling in the Word (15–20 minutes)

Have copies of Scripture available for everyone.

Have two people (male/female or adult/child) take turns reading the passage aloud.

- After the first reading, ask people to open themselves to the Spirit and focus on these questions:
  - In listening to the text, was there a phrase or word that stood out to you?
  - Are there words, phrases, or ideas that grasp you?
  - Is there a question you would like to ask?
- After the second reading, ponder the questions again.
- After several moments of silence, ask the group to share.
  - If a small group, ask the whole group to share together the questions below.
  - If a large group, break into smaller groups of two to three people and share within your small group. After sharing two minutes each, report to the larger group what your partner heard God say to the questions below.
  - Where did you stop? Why?
  - How did you hear God?
  - What new insights or questions emerged?
  - What does this passage have to do with living in Christian community?
  - What are you hearing God say in the midst of today's conversation?
- Finally, ask the group, "How are we hearing God's call to respond through our passage of Scripture in our context?"

Choose enough readings to navigate your table life group gatherings. Following are some suggestions.

Table Life
Eat: Isaiah 25:1-9; Revelation 22:1-5, 12-17
Dwell: Psalm 119:1-16, 33-48
Listen: Deuteronomy 6:1-12
Storytelling: Acts 26
Communion: Luke 22:7-38

Love God, Love Others
Mark 12:28-34
John 15:1-17
1 John 4:7-21
Colossians 3:1-17

Who God Is and Who I Am
Psalm 8
Psalm 24
Psalm 44 or Psalm 51
Psalm 113
Psalm 1–2

What Is the Gospel?
1 Corinthians 15:1-28
1 John 5:1-12
Romans 5:1-11
Hebrews 2:10–3:6

Forty Days
Moses: Exodus 34
Elijah: 1 Kings 19
Jesus: Matthew 4

Sermon on the Mount
Matthew 5
Matthew 6
Matthew 7

Read a Whole Book or Letter
Jonah 1–4
Ruth 1–4
Philippians 1–4
Colossians 1–4

NOTE

1. Adapted from Alan I. Roxburgh, *Joining God, Remaking Church, Changing the World: The New Shape of the Church in Our Time* (New York: Morehouse, 2015), 68–69.

Appendix B

Storytelling Guide

Eating together is a powerful experience. It connects us to one another in ways few other activities can. One of the greatest elements of any meal is conversation. It is how you learn more about others and how you share yourself with them. When Jesus and the early church gathered for meals, they discussed the deepest and most meaningful parts of life and faith.

To better connect with your table group and the church, it is important to share your story with others and to hear the stories of your fellow church community members. This is going to be an experience where trust and openness are encouraged.

During each gathering of your table groups, two members of the group will share their story. Each person should expect to share for approximately twenty minutes. Over the course of three meals, every participant will share their story. This is an important element of table life, so please do not skip over this portion of your meeting together.

To help you prepare to share your stories, some suggested topics to cover during your storytelling time are listed below.

Where did you grow up? Share a little about your growing-up family.

If you are married or dating, how did you meet your spouse or partner?

Share about your job or vocation.

What has been the greatest challenge of your life?

What has been the greatest joy of your life?

Are you a Christian? If so, how and when did you first realize you wanted to be a Christian? If you do not identify as a Christian, would you like to learn more about what it means to be Christian?

Why are you a member or participant of this church?

When did you first begin attending this church?

Where do you currently see God working in your life?

Where do you struggle seeing God actively working right now?

What is your favorite passage of Scripture?

What areas of Scripture do you struggle with?

What is one thing you want your table group to know about you that they may not already know?

Appendix C

Sharing Questions[1]

Sharing questions help group members become more familiar with the people in the group. It helps to shift members' focus from themselves and onto the group. It can also help stimulate an atmosphere of open sharing. Revealing ourselves to each other is important: each time we open the door to an area in our life, the group can now pray for us and encourage us to obey God in that area.

Sharing Questions on the Past

What was something you were good at as a child, and how did that make you feel?

Use one word to characterize yourself at some younger age. Does that word still apply to you today?

Tell three things about the home in which you grew up.

How did your family celebrate Christmas when you were in grade school?

Where did you live during first grade?

Where did you feel warm and safe as a child? (place or person)

Name one person from your childhood whom you admired. What was the quality?

What is a favorite childhood memory?

What was one of your struggles as a teenager?

If you had a time machine, what time would you go back to and why?

What is one of your favorite movies?

Tell about a turning point in your life.

What has been a significant spiritual experience of Jesus for you?

What person has had a great influence on your spiritual life?

When has God been very present with you?

Sharing Questions on the Present

What do you do on a typical Thursday?

What is one thing that gave you a sense of accomplishment this week?

If you live to age seventy-five, you will have 657,000 hours in your life. Looking back over the past month, identify an hour or two you spent wisely.

When this week did you feel close to God?

If you were given two extra hours per day, how would you use them?

Name one thing you really like about yourself.

Name one thing you would like God to change in yourself.

What's one of your least favorite ways to spend a vacation?

If you could vacation anywhere in the world, where would you go and why?

If Jesus were coming to your house for supper, what recent happening in your life would you like to thank Jesus for?

What room in your house do you like best?

Of all the teachings of Jesus Christ, what has come to be of great significance for you?

Whose approval, other than God's, do you need the most?

How do you tune into God?

How would you describe yourself to someone who does not know you?

What is a time during the week you can relax?

Tell us three things that happened to you today.

What are two of your strongest skills?

What would you be doing if you were not here?

What was an important thing that happened to you this past week?

Sharing Questions on the Future

If God could grant you a wish, what would it be?

If you found out you were near the end of your life, what unsaid words or unfinished deeds would you want to complete?

What would you like to be doing five years from now?

What would you do if you knew you couldn't fail?

When you are ten years older, what kind of person do you want to be?

What is something you think God wants you to do?

If you could do anything you want this time next year, what would it be?

What epitaph do you want on your tombstone?

Where would you live if you could move anywhere in the world and why?

What is one thing you would like to accomplish in the week ahead?

Tips When Using Sharing Questions

Introduce the question and launch it yourself. One problem with ice breakers is that they can take up the whole session. Stop this from happening by answering the sharing question yourself first and by not talking more than one or two sentences. Before continuing, you might say, "If each one of us takes no more than two minutes for our answer, we will each be able to share." If someone does talk too long, deliberately look at your watch.

Go around the circle. Otherwise the shy person will avoid saying anything.

Watch for crisis needs. It is not unusual for someone to signal they have a real hurt or problem during the sharing question. "I heard this week that my mother has cancer." Obviously, you must return to minister to this need . . . but do not stop the circle of sharing. Say, "We will come back to you and share more about that, Susan. Thanks for telling us." Then, continue and do come back. If, however, a group member's emotional scar cries for immediate prayer, then the rest of the agenda must wait.

NOTE

1. Used with permission from Dr. Jeff Savage, First Baptist Church, Springfield, Oregon.

Appendix D

Communion Liturgies

Liturgy 1

Have a leader read the light sections and the group respond by reading the bold.

Opening

Greeting

The Lord be with you.

And also with you.

Prayer of Thanksgiving

Offer a prayer of your own design or

Lord Jesus, we give you thanks for loving the world so much you took on flesh and bone and dwelled among us. Through your life, death, and resurrection you have redeemed the world you created. You have called us into new life. As we gather around this table to celebrate how you have restored creation through your sacrifice and resurrection, we ask that you would be present here among us. Open our eyes that we may see you in the bread and the cup and in the faces of those gathered around this table. Give us such an awareness of your grace and love that with thankful hearts we will praise you with every ounce of our being in word and in deed. In Jesus' name. **Amen.**

READING OF SCRIPTURE

Choose an appropriate Scripture passage or

The Lord Jesus on the night when he was betrayed took a loaf of bread, and when he had given thanks, he broke it and said,

"This is my body that is broken for you. Do this in remembrance of me."

In the same way, after the meal, he took the cup saying,

"This cup is the new covenant in my blood. Do this, each time you drink it, in remembrance of me."

For every time you eat bread and drink from the cup, you proclaim the Lord's death until he comes.

(based on 1 Corinthians 11:24-26)

SHARING OF THE BREAD AND THE CUP

Have a leader hold up the bread and say:

This is the body of Christ, broken for you.

Break the bread. Tear off a piece to keep; pass the bread to have each person tear off a piece in turn. As each person hands the bread to the next person at the table repeat ***"This is the body of Christ, broken for you."***

Have a leader hold up the cup and say:

This is the cup of the new covenant, Christ's blood shed for you.

Set the cup down. Have everyone in the group dip their bread into the cup and eat or pass the cup to be drunk individually. If you pass the cup from person to person do so with the blessing, ***"This is the cup of the new covenant, Christ's blood shed for you."***

Closing

Prayer

A closing prayer of your own design or

Lord Jesus, we give you thanks that you have refreshed our hearts, minds, and souls at your table by being present here with us. Continue to deepen our faith in you. Increase our love for one another. Send us out into the world you created with peace, love, and hope.

Amen.

Dismissal

The grace of the Lord Jesus Christ and the love of God and the power of the Holy Spirit be with us all. Let us go in perfect communion with Christ and one another.

Amen.

Liturgy 2

Have a leader read the light sections and the group respond by reading the bold.

Opening

Greeting

The Lord be with you.
And also with you.
Lift up your hearts.
We lift them to the Lord.
Let us give thanks to the Lord our God.
It is right to give him thanks and praise.

PRAYER OF THANKSGIVING

The leader gives thanks to God the Father for God's work in creation and the revelation of God to God's people through Jesus' incarnation and the eternal presence of the Holy Spirit. Prayer concludes with the gathered body saying together

Holy, Holy, Holy Lord, God of power and might, heaven and earth are full of your glory. Hosanna in the highest. Blessed is he who comes in the name of the Lord. Hosanna in the highest. Amen.

SONG

The group can choose to sing an appropriate song.

READING OF SCRIPTURE

One of the teachers of the law came and heard them debating. Noticing that Jesus had given them a good answer, he asked him,

"Of all the commandments, which is the most important?"

"The most important one," answered Jesus, "is this:

'Hear, O Israel: The Lord our God, the Lord is one. Love the Lord your God with all your heart and with all your soul and with all your mind and with all your strength.'

"The second is this:

'Love your neighbor as yourself. There is no commandment greater than these.'"

(Mark 12:28-31)

PRAYER OF CONFESSION

Most merciful God,
we confess that we have sinned against you
in thought, word, and deed,
by the things we have done,
and by the things we have left undone.

**We have not loved you with our whole heart;
we have not loved our neighbors as ourselves.
We are truly sorry and we humbly repent.
For the sake of your Son Jesus Christ,
have mercy on us and forgive us,
that we may delight in your will,
and walk in your ways,
to the glory of your Name. Amen.**

(Adapted from the Book of Common Prayer)

Sharing of the Bread and the Cup

Have a leader hold up the bread and say:

This is the body of Christ, broken for you.

Break the bread. Tear off a piece to keep; pass the bread to have each person tear off a piece in turn. As each person hands the bread to the next person at the table repeat, ***"This is the body of Christ, broken for you."***

Have a leader hold up the cup and say:

This is the cup of the new covenant, Christ's blood shed for you.

Set the cup down. Have everyone in the group dip their bread into the cup and eat or pass the cup to be drunk individually. If you pass the cup from person to person do so with the blessing, ***"This is the cup of the new covenant, Christ's blood shed for you."***

Closing

Prayer

A closing prayer of your own design or

Father, Son, and Holy Spirit, as you are in constant and perfect communion with one another, we seek to be in perfect communion with you and with those gathered around this table. Send us now into the world in peace. Guide us in the ways of loving you with our hearts, minds, and souls and loving our neighbors as we love ourselves.

Amen.

DISMISSAL

Let us go forth in the name of the Father, the Son, and the Holy Spirit.

Thanks be to God.

Go in peace to love and serve the Lord.

Thanks be to God.

Bibliography

Bausch, William J. *Storytelling: Imagination and Faith*. Mystic, CT: Twenty-Third Publications, 1984.

Blomberg, Craig. *Contagious Holiness: Jesus' Meals with Sinners*. New Studies in Biblical Theology 19. Downers Grove, IL: InterVarsity Press, 2005.

Bonhoeffer, Dietrich. *Life Together*. New York: HarperCollins, 2005.

Boyd, Danah. *It's Complicated: The Social Lives of Networked Teens*. New Haven: Yale University Press, 2014.

Bradshaw, Paul F., and Maxwell E. Johnson. *The Eucharistic Liturgies: Their Evolution and Interpretation*. Collegeville, MN: Liturgical Press, 2012.

Chester, Tim. *A Meal with Jesus: Discovering Grace, Community, and Mission around the Table*. Wheaton, IL: Crossway, 2011.

Collins, John J., and Daniel C. Harlow, eds. *The Eerdmans Dictionary of Early Judaism*. Grand Rapids, MI: Eerdmans, 2010.

Damiani, Aaron. *The Good of Giving Up: Discovering the Freedom of Lent*. Chicago, IL: Moody Publishers, 2017.

"Dinner with Jesus and Paul." The BAS Library, August 24, 2015. https://members.bib-arch.org/bible-review/20/4/7.

Earley, Justin Whitmel. *The Common Rule: Habits of Purpose for an Age of Distraction*. Downers Grove, IL: InterVarsity Press, 2019.

Fitch, David E. *Faithful Presence: Seven Disciplines That Shape the Church for Mission*. Downers Grove, IL: InterVarsity Press, 2016.

Frost, Michael. *Surprise the World: The Five Habits of Highly Missional People*. Colorado Springs, CO: NavPress, 2016.

Goldingay, John. *Reading Jesus's Bible: How the New Testament Helps Us Understand the Old Testament*. Grand Rapids, MI: Eerdmans, 2017.

Gorrell, Angela Williams. *Always On: Practicing Faith in a New Media Landscape*. Grand Rapids, MI: Baker Academic, 2019.

Heil, Emily. "Eating Alone, Together: Virtual Dinner Parties Are Helping People Fight Isolation." *Washington Post*, March 21, 2020, sec. 1. https://www.washingtonpost.com/news/voraciously/wp/2020/03/21/eating-alone-together-virtual-dinner-parties-are-helping-people-fight-isolation/.

Hellerman, Joseph H. *When the Church Was a Family: Recapturing Jesus' Vision for Authentic Christian Community*. Nashville, TN: B & H Academic, 2009.

Holt, Simon Carey. *Eating Heaven: Spirituality at the Table*. Brunswick, Australia: Acorn Press, 2013.

Jethani, Skye. "The case against sermon-centric Sundays," *Premier Christianity*, https://www.premierchristianity.com/Past-Issues/2019/October-2019/The-case-against-sermon-centric-Sundays.

Karris, Robert J. *Eating Your Way Through Luke's Gospel*. Collegeville, MN: Liturgical Press, 2006.

Kinnaman, David, and Mark Matlock. *Faith for Exiles: 5 Ways to Help a New Generation Follow Jesus and Thrive in Digital Babylon*. Grand Rapids, MI: Baker Academic, 2019.

Kreider, Alan. *The Patient Ferment of the Early Church: The Improbable Rise of Christianity in the Roman Empire*. Grand Rapids, MI: Baker Academic, 2016.

Lewis, C.S. *The Screwtape Letters*, Signature Classic. New York: HarperOne, 2015.

Malina, Bruce J. *The New Testament World: Insights from Cultural Anthropology*. 3rd ed. Louisville, KY: Westminster John Knox Press, 2001.

Matshe, Gertrude. "Ubuntu - a person is a person through other persons." YouTube video. 18:40. Posted by "Tedx Talks," August 3, 2013. https://www.youtube.com/watch?v=BzIyOtusDxE.

McGowan, Andrew B. *Ancient Christian Worship: Early Church Practices in Social, Historical, and Theological Perspective*. Grand Rapids, MI: Baker Academic, 2014.

McHugh, Adam S. *The Listening Life: Embracing Attentiveness in a World of Distraction*. Downers Grove, IL: InterVarsity Press, 2015.

McKnight, Scot. *A Fellowship of Differents: Showing the World God's Design for Life Together*. Grand Rapids, MI: Zondervan, 2015.

———. *The Blue Parakeet: Rethinking How You Read the Bible*. Grand Rapids, MI: Zondervan, 2008.

———. *One.Life: Jesus Calls, We Follow.* Grand Rapids, MI: Zondervan, 2010.

"Our Mission." The Bible Project. Accessed March 16, 2020. https://thebibleproject.com/about/.

Packiam, Glen. *Blessed Broken Given: How Your Story Becomes Sacred in the Hands of Jesus*. Colorado Springs, CO: Multnomah, 2019.

Peterson, Eugene H. *Christ Plays in Ten Thousand Places: A Conversation in Spiritual Theology*. Grand Rapids, MI: Eerdmans, 2008.

———. *The Contemplative Pastor: Returning to the Art of Spiritual Direction*. Grand Rapids, MI: Eerdmans, 1993.

———. *Five Smooth Stones for Pastoral Work*. Grand Rapids, MI: Eerdmans, 1992.

Ridgeway, Chris. "Online Communion Can Still Be Sacramental." ChristianityToday.com. Accessed April 13, 2020. https://www.christianitytoday.com/ct/2020/march-web-only/online-communion-can-still-be-sacramental.html.

Roxburgh, Alan J. *Joining God, Remaking Church, Changing the World: The New Shape of the Church in Our Time*. New York: Morehouse, 2015.

Sandnes, Karl Olav. *A New Family: Conversion and Ecclesiology in the Early Church with Cross-Cultural Comparisons*. Studien Zur Interkulturellen Geschichte Des Christentums, Etudes d'histoire Interculturelle Du Christianisme = Studies in the Intercultural History of Christianity, Bd. 91. Berne: Peter Lang, 1994.

Smith, C. Christopher, and John Pattison. *Slow Church: Cultivating Community in the Patient Way of Jesus*. Downers Grove, IL: InterVarsity Press, 2014.

Smith, Dennis E. *From Symposium to Eucharist: The Banquet in the Early Christian World*. Minneapolis, MN: Fortress Press, 2009.

Smith, James K. A. *Imagining the Kingdom: How Worship Works*. Cultural Liturgies, Vol. 2. Grand Rapids, MI: Baker Academic, 2013.

Sparks, Paul, Tim Sorens, and Dwight J. Friesen. *The New Parish: How Neighborhood Churches Are Transforming Mission, Discipleship and Community*. Downers Grove, IL: InterVarsity Press, 2014.

Sweet, Leonard I. *From Tablet to Table: Where Community Is Found and Identity Is Formed*. Colorado Springs, CO: NavPress, 2014.

Trebilco, Paul. *Self-Designations and Group Identity in the New Testament*. Cambridge: Cambridge University Press, 2012.

Tyson, Jon, and Heather Grizzle. *A Creative Minority: Influencing Culture through Redemptive Participation*. Self-published, 2016.

White, Dan. *Love Oover Fear: Facing Monsters, Befriending Enemies, and Healing Our Polarized World*. Chicago: Moody Publishers, 2019.

Willard, Dallas. *The Divine Conspiracy: Rediscovering Our Hidden Life in God*. 1st ed. San Francisco: HarperSanFrancisco, 1998.

Wright, N. T. "The Letter to the Ephesians." *Theology in Scotland* 20, no. 2 (2013): 5–7.